HYPERBOREA

And The Lost Age of Man

MICHAEL SZYMCZYK

Szymczyk, Michael, 1981-
Atlantis & Its Fate In The Postdiluvian World
Paperback ISBN: 9798336292398 | Hardcover ISBN: 9798336573862

This work is speculative entertainment, aiming to take some of the most absurd and outlandish stories from ancient history and explore them with an open mind and a sense of humor, considering whether they could have a scientific or technological basis that has evolved into myth over time. While meticulously researched and grounded in science, its purpose is to provide information often dismissed by mainstream narratives, offering explanations for descriptions in ancient writings that are frequently dismissed as fictional myths.

Designed as a resource for independent researchers who also aim to discover the lost land of Hyperborea, it compiles every mention of Hyperborea in ancient texts. Additionally, it provides a comprehensive list of potential locations and explores the possible connections between Hyperborea and the Druids, through figures like Abaris the Hyperborean and Pythagoras.

Additionally, the topic of Hyperborea, like Atlantis, has often been tainted by associations with extremist, nationalist and racist ideologies, which prevents serious academic inquiry and research. This book does not support such ideologies and encourages those who do to reconsider, as a study of mankind's origins reveals that, when one goes far back enough in time, we find we all come from the same family.

Table of Contents

"*Let's be honest with ourselves. We are Hyperboreans; we know how far removed we are from others. 'Neither by land nor by sea will you find the way to the Hyperboreans'—Pindar already knew this about us. Beyond the north, beyond ice and death—that's where we find our life and happiness. We have discovered happiness; we know the way; we've found the exit from the labyrinth of thousands of years. Has anyone else found it? Modern man, perhaps? 'I am lost; I am everything that has become lost,' sighs modern man. This modernity was our illness: lazy peace, cowardly compromise, the whole unclean virtue of the modern Yes and No. Better to live in the ice than among modern virtues and other mild climates! We were brave enough; we didn't spare ourselves or others; but for a long time, we didn't know where to channel our strength. We became gloomy; people called us fatalists. Our fate—abundance, tension, the build-up of power. We thirsted for lightning and action and were far from the happiness of the weakling and their 'resignation.' A storm brewed in our atmosphere; our nature became dark—for we saw no path forward. Our formula for happiness: a Yes, a No, a straight line, a goal.*"

Friedrich Nietzsche

Preface

In the last ten thousand years, the human brain has shrunk by up to 15%. People in 8,000 BCE generally had brains that were much larger than ours, and having a bigger brain during prehistoric times was not just limited to our species. Contrary to the stereotype of the Neanderthals as primitive and unintelligent, they possessed brain sizes comparable and even larger than prehistoric men, averaging around 1,500 to 1,700 cubic centimeters (compared to our current brain size of 1,350 cubic centimeters). Our lesser-known cousins, the Denisovans, are believed to have had even larger brains, and there might be other offshoots of humanity waiting to be discovered by archaeologists with even larger cranial capacities. However, mainstream scientific narratives often overlook these details, perhaps because they challenge the assumption that civilization began only six thousand years ago with the Sumerians. This view implies that a larger brain does not necessarily correlate with higher intelligence, as it assumes that earlier hominids failed to develop civilization, writing, science, and other hallmarks of advanced society.

But what if the current scientific consensus and our understanding of prehistory is fundamentally flawed? For instance, the Sumerians documented in their records that civilization had existed for hundreds of thousands of years before their own time, suggesting that they did not view themselves as the first advanced culture. According to the Sumerian King List, there were rulers who reigned for extraordinarily long periods before a great flood, hinting at a belief in a much older and possibly advanced civilization that was wiped away after the last Ice Age. Could it be that ancient civilizations existed, superior to our own, and that have since been erased from memory and buried by geological time?

If so, could our current Western Civilization not be the pinnacle of human development but rather a result of de-evolution and a decline in overall intelligence? The notion that a sign of intelligence in geological records will be marked by radioactive waste, plastics, and other pollutants may not signify intelligence at all. Instead, it could indicate a failure to harmonize with the environment—a sign of a species prioritizing short-term gains over long-term sustainability. An intelligent species, one might argue, would avoid environmental destruction, war, animal cruelty, and the creation of non-biodegradable materials, opting instead for a path that fosters harmony with the natural world. In pursuit of sustainability, they might explore alternatives, such as the manipulation of spacetime, which could potentially eliminate the need for traditional agriculture and animal consumption. For instance, instead of relying on conventional farming or the needless slaughter of animals, they might develop innovative means of sustenance, such as bioengineering and cultivating specific molds that could provide nourishment without the ecological footprint of traditional agriculture, and ensuring that their existence and progress do not come at the expense of the environment or other living beings.

The reduction in brain size in our species has been attributed to various factors, including environmental changes. Around 12,000 years ago, the planet experienced a sudden warming, leading to significant climatic shifts. This warming trend resulted in a dramatic rise in sea levels by approximately 400 feet since that time. Some scientists believe that this environmental shift may have contributed to the gradual reduction in brain size, as the challenges of heat dissipation in warmer climates might have influenced evolutionary pressures. The future, marked by accelerating global warming, warns of a continuation of this trend. As the planet heats up, there is a risk that human cognitive abilities may increasingly diminish, potentially leading to a society where humanity becomes even more stupid and barbaric. This assumes, of course, that any significant portion of our species survives beyond small pockets of hunter-gatherer communities, which may be all that remains after the collapse of Western Civilization. Such a collapse is likely inevitable, caused by short-sighted resource management, a blind consumption of fossil fuels over renewables, a society that indoctrinates its young to value war, murder, cruelty and violence over learning, thoughtfulness, empathy and compromise, and a primitive economic system that prioritizes the wealth of a small minority while simultaneously allowing the least capable and intelligent individuals among us to hold positions of power.

Regardless of the fate of humanity, one thing is certain: as humans migrated north, their brains tended to increase in size, while those who returned to warmer climates often saw a reduction in brain mass. This phenomenon can be attributed to the brain's metabolism and the challenges of heat dissipation. Larger brains require more energy and generate more heat, making them less favorable in hot environments. Evolutionary processes likely favored smaller brains in such climates as a way to better manage thermal regulation.

Now, let's consider the possibility that the argument stating "the size of the brain does not directly correlate with intelligence" may need to be reexamined, as it could be fundamentally flawed, and that there could have been groups in our prehistory with greater intellectual, memorization and reasoning abilities than even our brightest minds today, and which would likely have originated in colder regions, where cranial capacities and neocortical regions of the brain would be much larger. Tens of thousands of years ago, a civilization could have developed and flourished in the far northern and southern reaches of our planet—regions such as Beringia, Siberia, Canada, Antarctica, and areas now submerged underwater. These regions could have hosted people with cranial capacities much larger than ours, and a civilization which developed a science far more advanced than our own. As of now, this is merely speculative, but, for argument's sake, how could we investigate such a hypothesis? The first step would involve examining historical records and ancient texts for any references to these potential civilizations, and indeed, there are such references. The Gaelic myths of the Tuatha de Danann, Kumari Kandam in the Tamil tradition, the Apkallu in Sumerian mythology, the Aztecs' Aztlan, Plato's legendary city of Atlantis, and the Hyperboreans—all of these and more feature fantastical descriptions. While mainstream academia often views these accounts as purely mythical, they may, in fact, represent the remnants of an oral history that once described civilizations with advanced science and technology. Over time, these stories may have evolved into the myths and legends we know today, preserving fragments of lost knowledge about the world and its ancient peoples. The challenge, however, lies in discerning which narratives might be rooted in actual history rather than pure imagination. One approach to addressing this challenge is to critically review ancient historical texts, re-examining prior interpretations or translations. By doing so, we might uncover errors or biases that have obscured the original meanings. This method was effectively employed by Heinrich Schliemann, who used Homer's epics to locate the ancient city of Troy.

The second step involves conducting field research to search for signs of these lost civilizations in remote

areas based on our readings of ancient texts. For example, investigating archaeological sites with characteristics similar to those found in Arkaim or the Sundurun megaliths as shown in the images here, dated to around 2000 BCE. These sites feature distinctive architectural elements and alignments, suggesting a sophisticated understanding of astronomy, and a possible link to the proto Indo-European figure of Yemo, the god of death and the underworld, which later become Remus in the Roman tradition and Yema in the Indic civilizations.

Arkaim is often associated as a possible site of a Hyperborean civilization, and others have suggested the Hyperboreans might have had connections to the Druids and other priestly castes in ancient times. The term priestly, however, might be a misnomer, these castes may have rather been the intelligentsia, who developed and transmitted ancient sources of knowledge and a science based on quantum physics via an oral tradition which has now been lost to time. The one true faith may, in fact, have been science.

One reason the idea of ancient civilizations in these regions is often dismissed is due to the logistical challenges associated with exploring these harsh and remote areas, not to mention how expensive it is. Furthermore, the passage of geological time would have likely erased most physical traces, especially if these civilizations were advanced and lived in harmony with their environment. This way of life also would have left little impact on the landscape, making it even more difficult to collect physical evidence. As a result, serious research within this field has been sparse, and those with open minds who actively seek evidence to support it are even more rare. However,

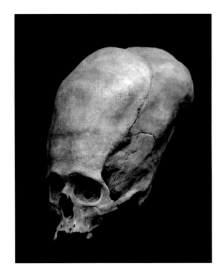

this does not mean there is no evidence to consider. For instance, the Paracas skulls found in South America are a strange, but blindly dismissed, anomaly. These elongated skulls date back thousands of years and show genetic markers that suggest an ancestry linked to Eastern Europe and the Levant, specifically, Mesopotamia. Some of the skulls have red hair, and other features which suggest artificial cranial deformation was not responsible for the elongation. How did these people come to South America around 800 BCE? Could these skulls be remnants of a migration from a long-lost civilization?

In exploring this hypothesis, the legend of Hyperborea comes to mind, an ancient place believed by the Greeks to exist at the edge of the known world, beyond where the cold wind of Boreas blows. Could these skulls be evidence of a Hyperborean civilization, one that navigated the globe and made contact with distant lands like South America? Further supporting the existence of ancient, possibly technologically advanced civilizations are discoveries of large mummified remains and anomalous skulls. Notably, the Lovelock Cave skulls in Nevada dated to around 2,000 to 4,000 years ago, with their unusually large size, suggest a potentially distinct and advanced human lineage. In Alaska, the Aleutian Islands have yielded skulls that indicate cranial capacities far exceeding those of modern humans. On Kagamil Island, a skull was discovered with an estimated cranial capacity of 2,000 cubic centimeters. Despite evidence of its transfer to the Smithsonian Institution, the skull inexplicably vanished from official records.

Similarly, in 1940 on the island of Shemya, military personnel uncovered more skulls and bones while constructing an airstrip. Some of these remains reportedly exhibited cranial capacities two to three times

larger than those of contemporary humans. However, when biologist Ivan Sanderson sought to investigate these findings, he found that the remains had mysteriously disappeared, much like the skull from Kagamil Island. It was reported that the Shemya remains were handed over to academic institutions, only to disappear without a trace. If you search online for information about this, you will find very little to no documentation. It appears that the records have been removed or were never made publicly accessible.

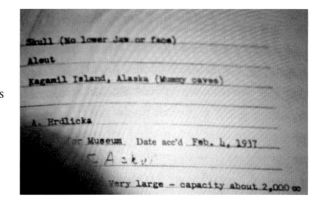

However, evidence such as the documentation for the Kagamil Island skull still exists as shown here, raising an important question: why are certain individuals at institutions like the Smithsonian—an organization many consider trustworthy—possibly removing evidence from the public domain? This situation suggests the possibility of intentional obfuscation or suppression of information, preventing public access to potentially significant archaeological findings.

Additionally, the elongated skulls found in Malta, dating back to as early as 4,000 BCE, and in other megalithic cultures, may indicate a group with unique genetic traits and a distinct lineage separate from other populations of the time. This brings up the question as to whether they could have migrated there from elsewhere, but if so, where?

Ancient texts, including those by Plato, reference the Hyperboreans, a legendary people believed to have traveled to Greece in very small numbers, in a manner that could be viewed similarly to those of a modern day religious missionary. Could it be possible that they traveled even further than Greece, leaving behind these anomalous skulls and genetic markers as evidence of their existence?

This idea suggests that the Hyperboreans, or a similar advanced group, may have left traces of their presence across different regions, including Europe and the Americas. These traces could manifest as the unusual skull shapes and sizes found in places like the Aleutian Islands, the American Southwest, Peru and Malta, indicating a distinct lineage with potentially advanced knowledge or abilities.

As for Hyperborea, the legend of this land first captivated my interest during my research for *Atlantis & Its Fate In The Postdiluvian World*. In that book, I proposed a solution to the enigma of Plato's Atlantis using a common sense approach. All known copies of Plato's dialogues are translations, not the Ancient Greek originals, which were lost to time. The story of Atlantis, relayed to Solon by an Ammonean priest in Egypt, suggests that rather than following a literal translation of Plato (which has likely been corrupted) we should examine Ancient Egyptian texts about lost lands instead to see what they wrote down, and look at other evidence, such as genetic, linguistic and other historical accounts. One place in particular that might fit within the Ancient Egyptian literature is Aaru, or the Field of the Reeds. In addition, Plato substituted Greek names over the Ancient Egyptian originals, which in my opinion likely

lead to translation errors by later Roman, Arabic, and Medieval scholars.

Several key misinterpretations could have involved the word for Hercules as a replacement for Heryshaf, Horus, Shu or another figure in Ancient Egyptian mythology. It is quite possible as well the Pillars referenced in Plato's original Ancient Greek text were originally meant as a concept related to Aaru, as shown in the image from the Papyrus of Ani that depicts a staircase between a temple entrance that depicts pillars, as well as an "ark" containing stones on a boat as well as two other boats also featuring staircases (*I've been informed by a professional researcher on the subject that the colored objects are most likely an artistic representation of food placed on an offering table; and that the Ark of the Covenant was likely inspired by the usage of Ancient Egyptian solar barques).* The concept of pillars is also present in Chinese mythology, particularly in their depiction of the "pillars of heaven." One creation myth tells of a catastrophic event when one of these pillars was broken, leading to widespread floods, fires, and stars falling from the sky, nearly resulting in the destruction of the Earth.

One of the reasons no one has found Atlantis in my opinion is that interpolations and misinterpretations of the Ancient Egyptian originals likely caused people to follow a literal translation of Plato that takes them west of Europe or in the Mediterranean rather than what the original Egyptian writings had probably put down if the legend of Atlantis was inspired by their belief in Aaru. Then, of course, Plato also wrote of Γάδειρα or "Gades," which may have been a translator's replacement for Ἅδης or "Hades," especially if one imagines a copyist replacing the terms believing it to be a prior error. Aaru, to the Ancient Egyptians, was known as the homeland of Osiris in Egyptian records, and would have been similar to the Ancient Greek concept for Hades and the Underworld. If we consider the Egyptian concept of Aaru, the *Land of the Dead* located far to the east, it becomes apparent that translators with limited geographic knowledge might have altered the narrative to fit one within their own cultural context, specifically, a Roman or Medieval one. This misunderstanding could explain why searches for Atlantis that have focused westward of Egypt have come up empty, which is because they have ignored the actual location to the east especially when all other evidence is considered. Other stories in Ancient Egyptian texts, such as *The Shipwrecked Sailor*, suggest this land may have had connections to the Land of Punt, from where the Egyptians believed their gods originated. In addition, that story features an island that sinks into the ocean, and a serpent that speaks of a star that struck the island, killing its relatives. Other historical evidence, along with anomalous X2 haplogroup genetic markers and various linguistic connections, suggests that Atlantis—or Aaru—may have remained undiscovered due to misinterpretations rooted in later translations and the dismissals of many skeptics who lacked any understanding of Ancient Egyptian beliefs. The R in Ancient Egyptian can also be translated as L or N, implying that Aaru could have been spoken of as Aalu or Aanu. The ancient historian Manetho wrote of an ancient line of Egyptian kings known as the *Auriteans (or Auliteans/Auniteans)*, which might support the idea they came from Aaru. It is my belief this civilization, if it existed, was located in Beringia, near a caldera southeast of Chirikof Island that was destroyed in a cataclysmic event around 9,600 BCE.

Plato mentions a group the Atlanteans fought against, and who, it is suggested in his dialogue, were connected in ancient times to both the Athenians and the priestly caste in Sais, Egypt. I wondered if perhaps Hyperborea might have connections to that civilization, or perhaps, the group that fought Atlantis?

Interestingly enough, the ancient Greek historian Herodotus placed Hyperborea in this general direction, towards Siberia, and Pliny the Elder, noted some accounts that believed it was in Northeast

Asia, not too far from where I believe Plato's lost city of Atlantis might be located. Could they, along with other myths such as the Chinese myth of Mount Penglai or the Japanese myth of Hōrai, somehow be connected through a much more ancient source that comes to us now only through myth and legend?

However, the dates of Atlantis and Hyperborea don't fit. Some writers mistakenly place Hyperborea in the same era as Plato's Atlantis and suggest these two powers were at war, while many others have adjusted the timeline of Atlantis to be closer to that of Troy, arguing that Plato's original date is implausible. Yet, if we take ancient authors at their word, Atlantis existed around 10,000 BCE, give or take a few centuries, while Hyperborea is generally dated to between the 13th and 6th centuries BCE. This discrepancy makes it unlikely that Hyperborea was the nation that defeated Atlantis, unless our understanding of the timeline or the nature of Hyperborea's existence—such as its geographical location or duration—is incorrect.

And yet, despite this apparent incongruity, I still wondered if there might be some connection to the story Plato tells us in the Critias and Timaeus? Some of the descriptions of Hyperboreans which have survived are so fantastic to the point most consider them unbelievable legends, but what if those descriptions were due to an advanced knowledge of science, medicine and technology that had its source from an antediluvian civilization such as Atlantis, or the nation that defeated them? The story of Abaris the Hyperborean, who reportedly flew around the world using an arrow gifted from Apollo, brings to mind either a person flying in a jet or even a picture of a witch riding a broomstick, not something anyone takes seriously until you consider the possibility that what was considered magic might have actually been artifacts and techniques initially engineered via a science based upon quantum physics (and the manipulation of alloys which express quantum effects when stimulated in a certain way). If so, then could it be that antediluvian technologies once existed but over the last two thousand years were destroyed by religious authorities, and before then, were only known and exploited by a select few who guarded it as a secret passed down from a much earlier, and now lost age of man? Even more interesting are the descriptions of Abaris the Hyperborean, who was said by Herodotus to have not eaten on his journey across the world on his arrow, which mirrors his description of the *Atlantes*: who were also said to eat no living thing.

In any case, such associations, while suggestive, remain entirely speculative, so the goal of my research was to investigate if there was anything more to the legend of Hyperborea which might connect the two? Plato's description of Poseidon arriving on a mountain in his dialogue about Atlantis opened up, at least to me, the possibility of a precursor civilization, one which preceded Atlantis and was extremely technologically advanced, and for which no records remain outside of the Sumerians and Ancient Egyptians (which are generally not considered historically accurate by modern academia). Many experts will dispute claims of advanced prehistoric civilizations and chalk it up to crazy talk, but in Platos' own words, he describes the figure of Poseidon not requiring a ship in a time when there were no boats, which brings to mind the legend of Abaris using an arrow to travel across the world. Is it so fallacious to ask if perhaps this description of Poseidon was based on actual history passed down to the Ancient Egyptians, and these so-called gods were but men that had developed advanced antigravity technology based on principles modern science is not yet fully aware of, or that have been suppressed by military authorities?

Fantastic descriptions in Plato's writings, such as a wall of Atlantis glowing with the red light of orichalchum, made me wonder if perhaps the character of Poseidon in Plato's story was a human utilizing advanced technology that came from a civilization far more ancient than the Sumerians, perhaps from around the Altai region of Siberia where dogs were believed to have been first domesticated. But of course, if there were such a civilization, one more technologically advanced than our own, we'd have likely found evidence for it by now, right?

Well, the problem with that is threefold: first, if an Ice Age civilization existed along coastal areas, it would now be submerged due to the significant rise in sea levels over the past 10,000 years. As a result, these potential archaeological sites remain largely inaccessible and unexplored. Second, if researchers operate under the assumption that we are the first technologically advanced civilization on Earth, they may not actively seek evidence to the contrary. This bias can lead to the dismissal of any anomalous findings as mere oddities or misinterpretations, rather than considering them as possible indicators of advanced ancient cultures. Lastly, academics who entertain such unconventional theories risk damaging their reputations and careers, which can discourage open-minded exploration and discussion of these possibilities. Consider how some skeptics treat Graham Hancock, subjecting him to Inquisition-style attacks akin to those faced by Giordano Bruno, merely for advocating the exploration of evidence and the pursuit of scientific research rather than strictly adhering to established dogmatic beliefs. Hancock advocates for re-examining established narratives about ancient civilizations and listening to what those civilizations themselves had to say, encouraging an open-minded approach to history and archaeology. However, his ideas face rejection and criticism from the academic community, with detractors dismissing his theories as fringe or pseudoscientific, rather than engaging with them as potential avenues for further investigation. This reaction highlights the challenge of proposing alternative perspectives in fields where conventional views are deeply entrenched. For example, some of the great Native American mounds near St. Louis, Missouri, were initially misattributed to natural geological formations and dismissed by the academic establishment. It wasn't until someone challenged this conventional view that the idea of these structures being man-made gained acceptance—an idea that was initially considered outrageous by many at the time. Secondly, it assumes that the byproducts of such an antediluvian civilization would resemble our own technological and cultural foundations. This perspective overlooks the possibility that an ancient civilization could have developed around entirely different principles, much like how Buddhism presents a unique worldview and societal structure. Thirdly, it presumes that we would immediately recognize such technology as advanced. In reality, it might require specific knowledge or conditions to activate—similar to the Was Scepter of Ancient Egypt, the Godstone of the Inishkea Islands in Ireland, or the mythical Philosopher's Stone. These artifacts and concepts suggest that advanced technologies or practices might have existed in forms unfamiliar to modern science and could easily be overlooked or misunderstood. Technology that harnesses materials with unique properties at the molecular and atomic levels, and requires specific sounds or vibrations to activate its quantum effects, might appear primitive to those unfamiliar with its true nature. Such technology could be as simple as a wooden staff or a rock, resembling Stone or Bronze Age artifacts. However, without knowledge of the precise methods needed to unlock their potential, these items could be easily misinterpreted as rudimentary tools.

In the book *Atlantis & Its Fate In The Postdiluvian World*, I suggested that it is possible an ancient technologically advanced culture with links to Plato's Atlantis has survived to the present day. Such a civilization could escape detection using time dilating technology (seen in our reports of UAPs and UFOs, so-called aliens, bigfoot and other paranormal activity and myths concerning fairies, elves, angels, gods and so on). This technology would make it so that one second of our time would be hours or even days in their time, allowing them to move around and interact with us without us even knowing, or having any way to detect them without using specialized high-speed cameras (though perhaps, other signs may present themselves, such as feeling a cool draft of air or finding cords to electronics seemingly tangled up in knots which we overlook as spontaneous knotting but which to others might very well be a humorous activity to play on their unsuspecting, and far less intelligent cousins). It should be noted that a truly advanced civilization would be able to live in places we do not suspect or would be able to detect without the proper know-how and equipment. Such a culture would have every reason to avoid contact with our civilization. A truly evolved society might look down on us as we look down on chimpanzees, and interact with us much as we do with wild animals we deem unpredictable and dangerous: from a comfortable distance and only physically interacting when we are either tranquilized or restrained. If they have developed technology which dilates not only time, but space, they could indeed be the "mound-dwellers" of our fairy tales, using technology capable of shrinking their spatial imprint so they are the size of insects or even smaller, with cities in the earth, ocean or sky that to an outside observer might only appear the size of a small rock or perhaps, mistaken for a cloud, moving satellite or rainbow glow in the sky. They may utilize genetically engineered bodies or suits with wings to fly in the air, the effects of gravity nullified with their technology, as discussed in the section of this book on Viktor Grebbenikov's claim of building a flying machine using the chitin of an endangered insect species in Siberia.

Having said that, if such a civilization were to exist, it is quite possible they have records or an oral history that go far beyond our own, and would be able to provide us with knowledge from a lost age of man that was wiped away either by war or a natural calamity, or perhaps was an age not even of men, but of a more evolved, or genetically engineered, ancestor of *homo sapiens* or another species unknown to us as of now in the anthropological record. It should be noted, this is not mere wild speculation, but a hypothesis generated from mummified remains that have been dismissed by the scientific establishment, anecdotal reports from whistle-blowers and a wealth of video and photographic evidence of things seen and reported by reputable witnesses for which no natural explanation has been able to account for.

It is my opinion, most importantly, that if such a civilization existed *and very likely even still exists*, it is quite possible that they could be responsible for the human belief in an afterlife, especially within the Ancient Egyptian traditions, and where human consciousness at the moment of death is preserved as information and perhaps for some, transferred to genetically engineered lifeforms, capable of living in a time and spatially dilated environment and who become, for lack of a better expression, immortal, and where others continue to exist purely as information, and others consigned to oblivion. The writings of the Ancient Egyptians and especially those of Hermes Trismegistus, if there is any truth to the literature of the *Corpus Hermeticum* originating in remote ancient Egyptian antiquity, could be a window into such a reality, but more on that in the last part of this book.

As an existential atheist, the thought of defending claims to a mystical afterlife is abhorrent because in my opinion, most religions are built on embracing ignorance and a refusal to question or look at evidence. To the rational mind, they are simply made up stories with no basis in fact or reality. However, if religions provide a doorway to more ancient sources of knowledge from a lost age of man with technology and knowledge far more advanced than our own, what we can then ask is whether there might exist a scientific explanation for how an afterlife might have been developed by an ancient unknown precursor civilization that exists to this day, and which seeded ancient religions with ideas that are not as outlandish when understood in the proper scientific, technological and historical context. This would not be a true afterlife as conceived by religious authorities, but a technologically driven one where consciousness and one's personality is preserved at the moment of death as information, and able to be transplanted into genetically engineered bodies that do not age, do not require oxygen, food, and have been engineered to exist in a high radiation, low light or infrared environment that is likely to occur in a time dilated environment; an underworld, so to speak. All of these things would have a physical basis in reality, and could, much like anything else, be scientifically verified with the right know-how, equipment and determination.

If such a precursor civilization existed or still exists, then clues to its existence might be gained by an investigation of mythical lands, which if real, could allow for the collection of evidence and artifacts to reconstruct a deeper understanding of *homo sapiens* prehistory, one which contained an epoch far different and yet more advanced than our own, and which has become in the last several millennia: *a lost age of man*.

It is possible that civilizations thousands of years in the future may view our era as a dark age, stretching from 9,000 BCE to the present, during which our true history was lost to time, awaiting rediscovery. This book serves several purposes: first, it is a quest to uncover this lost epoch, providing references to ancient authors on Hyperborea, which may have connections to this period before *our* recorded history. It then examines ancient writings and monuments suggestive of advanced technology, possibly utilizing antigravitational techniques that have either been lost over the millennia or suppressed by religious authorities and governments. The book explores the plausibility of such technology and how we might reconstruct it using any clues left in myths, legends and other stories, and proposes a wild hypothesis that there may be artifacts from ancient times capable of dilating spacetime. This theory suggests these relics utilized organic technology, akin to those that may have been developed by evolution within certain insects, where time dilation would confer evolutionary advantages such as reduced metabolic costs, predator avoidance, regenerative abilities, and enhanced flight capabilities. The final part of this book will also cover the necessary precautions one must take to enter into a time dilated environment, where those who master such technology, should it prove real, would find themselves like Orpheus descending into the Underworld.

For some readers, some of the contents of this book will be dismissed as pseudoscientific nonsense. I am not writing to change those opinions but to ask questions in the spirit of Socrates and to present information that is often overlooked by mainstream academics and the media, and thus unknown to the general public. Pseudoscience does exist, characterized by baseless claims and emotional rhetoric over reason and evidence. However, many skeptics of lost civilizations often conflate legitimate fringe hypotheses with truly pseudoscientific claims, using ridicule rather than reason to avoid engaging with the evidence. They may dismiss ideas they disagree with, employing a pseudo-scientific certitude that is not rooted in the scientific method. However, ridicule is not a substitute for rational inquiry and certainty is never guaranteed even for the most well argued position. Science should be about generating hypotheses, collecting evidence and making rational conjectures to explain phenomena we do not fully understand. It should not involve blindly dismissing ideas simply because they challenge our understanding or because we lack personal experience with them.

This book is not just about exploring hypotheses and presenting information though; it is also a guide on how and where to collect evidence to validate these ideas. It serves as a compilation to every reference to Hyperborea from ancient writers and presents a list of potential archaeological sites and historical anomalies that align with these descriptions, offering an opportunity for further exploration and research. *Hyperborea & The Lost Age of Man* requires an open mind and challenges readers to question the established narratives we have been taught. It also suggests that some evidence may be deliberately kept from public view by governments and religious authorities, who may wish to suppress a past that threatens their power and authority. The only way to uncover any evidence that has not been destroyed or hidden is to explore places untouched by these forces, such as the seafloor around Chirikof Island or the sites discussed later in this book.

It is my hope that such a journey to find Hyperborea could lead to the rediscovery of a science from a lost age of man, based on quantum physics, but repressed by those whom it would damage or who would not be able to profit from it. The idea of an energy free future where war and poverty are virtually non-existent would be castrating to those in power today, who utilize artificial divisions, indoctrination and debt to create a slave class that believes itself free and which serves its masters well by blindly believing everything it is taught and told. The idea that Hyperborea is a myth, which has endlessly been taught by the educational factories of our day, is therefore, like everything else we have been told to accept as fact, something we should all seriously cast doubt upon and question.

Part 1: On The Legend of Hyperborea

"Myth is much more important and true than history. History is just journalism and you know how reliable that is."

Joseph Campbell

Academics will tell you that Hyperborea is a mythical place that did not exist, and for good reason, there is no current archaeological evidence to support the existence of Hyperborea. This lack of evidence can be attributed to a general reluctance to search for something widely considered fictional. The skepticism surrounding Hyperborea also stems from the confused and contradictory nature of the references found in ancient writings, making it difficult to distinguish myth from reality. Any casual review of these works will likely lead to the same opinion; that it was *terra incognita* hearsay. However, the inconsistencies between ancient authors regarding Hyperborea should not lead us to automatically dismiss every mention of it as purely fictional. While it may not have been a kingdom in the traditional sense, like those of the Hittites, Hattians, or Kaskians, Hyperborea could have been a real place with a distinct cultural identity. It may have been a region inhabited by people like Abaris the Hyperborean, whose cultural and perhaps even physical migrations influenced the stories and myths passed down through the ages. These accounts might reflect genuine encounters or memories of a unique cultural group rather than purely mythical constructs. For example, we do have some descriptions of Hyperboreans. Accounts suggest that the Hyperboreans might have been exceptionally tall, dressed like Scythians and that they were free of the ravages of aging and disease. Aelius Herodianus, a 3rd-century grammarian, and Stephanus of Byzantium, writing a few centuries later, noted that the Arimaspi were similar in physical appearance to the Hyperboreans. Herodianus described them as being nearly identical in appearance. The Arimaspi were characterized as having fair hair by the poet Callimachus. So, we have a general idea, however beyond this, there is nothing in ancient texts that could help identify the physical traits of the Hyperboreans: *adding to the mystery*. Another challenge might even be misidentification with a group already known, this gulf between what the Greeks named things and what other cultures referred to themselves is a conundrum for any archaeologist hoping to discover Hyperborea. And indeed, one of the largest discrepancies is between those authors that place Hyperborea in Siberia, east of the Sythians, and those that may place them in regions near the British Isles. Some writers even believe that Pseudo-Apollodorus suggests a location to the south near ancient Libya as a location for Hyperborea

based on the mythological location of Atlas, adding to the confusion. The map to the right is Herodotus' map of the known world, where he places the Massagetes, Issedones, Arimaspians and Hyperboreans east of the Caspian Sea.

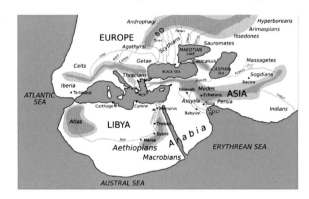

The most consistent element in all of the sources, however, is the association with a place just beyond the reach of the known world.

Given the disparate accounts, it's understandable why many view Hyperborea as a myth. There might be one solution to this conundrum though: the idea that all of these ancient authors were referring to the same group of people, a population that had spread from Siberia to places as far apart as the British Isles to the Tarim Basin, and became associated in later times with the Druids. The lack of direct evidence concerning the Druids leaves this hypothesis in the realm of rational speculation. Still, recorded connections between Pythagoras and Abaris the Hyperborean, alongside similarities between Pythagorean and Druidic beliefs, suggest a possible link. If we consider the Druids as a learned class that later coexisted with other populations, including Early European Farmer and Indo-European groups like the Celts, it could explain how ancient sources perceived Hyperboreans as spanning a broad northerly region, including both to the west and to the east of Greece.

If we entertain the notion that the Hyperboreans were a real people and were connected to a shamanic class that migrated to other lands, it also stands to reason that their culture must have had an original homeland from which they migrated from. In such a case, the lack of archaeological evidence is likely due to the site being buried and hidden much like the ancient city of Troy. If so, knowing where to look might be a good starting point for future archaeological discoveries especially since the location of Hyperborea in these conflicting ancient sources is where the waters become extremely murky.

So, *where do we look?* Heinrich Schliemann, the famed businessman turned archaeologist, consulted the writings of Homer in order to find the location of Troy, and indeed, one of the earliest mentions we have of Hyperborea is also from Homer. However, the work which contained this reference to Hyperborea, the *Epigoni*, is lost, and even its authorship by Homer was in doubt by the ancient Greek historian Herodotus.

Some details of the Epigoni have survived that could perhaps shed light on the age in which the Ancient Greeks believed Hyperborea existed. It is said that the Epigoni involves stories from the war of the Seven against Thebes, which was said to have taken place prior to the Trojan War, and the two Theban wars were considered by Hesiod to be two of the most important events that took place during the Age of Heroes, or the Fourth Age of Mankind. Beyond that there is little to be gained except speculation. However, this would mean Hyperborea existed prior to the 12th century BCE if one assumes the Trojan War took place around 1,194 BCE and that the Epigoni contained historically valid references to Hyperborea that would put it in that time.

A work similar in nature to the Epigoni, the Homeric Hymns, does survive, and in it a pirate speaks about the god Dionysus he has captured:

> "As for this fellow we men will see to him: I reckon he is bound for Egypt or for Cyprus or to the Hyperboreans or further still."

This might suggest a course north of Cyprus, perhaps an area around the Black Sea or beyond. However, it provides no definitive direction or location and as such, is not very helpful. Fragments from

Hesiod, in his Catalogs of Women, believed to be from around the 8th century BCE, also reference Hyperborea:

> "The winged Boreades chased the Harpies around the world. The Boreades flew
> swiftly in circles around them...among the well-horsed Hyperboreans—whom
> Gaea, the Earth, the life-giver, gave birth to far away by the tumbling rivers of
> deep-flowing Eridanos...of amber, nourishing her widely spread children."

From Hesiod's surviving description, there is little to be gained as to an actual location. The Hyperboreans are here depicted as having horses, and situated by a deep flowing river called the Eridanos (not to be confused with the Danube River, which the Ancient Greeks called Istros, which they borrowed from the Sythians, with its root in Sanskrit Isiras, meaning *swift*). As such, a location adjacent to a river by the Black Sea should be considered, but as noted above, the Danube might have been referred to by its proper name.

According to Asen Bondzhev, who has authored a wide-ranging paper on the ancient sources that wrote of Hyperborea, **Alcman**, a choral lyric poet from Sparta in the second half of the 7th century BC, is believed to have possibly used Aristeas of Proconnesus as a source, as they were contemporaries. Although Alcman's fragments do not explicitly mention the Hyperboreans, he is the first known author to mention the Riphean Mountains, often associated with remote peoples like the Issedones and Scythian horses. **Alcaeus**, another poet from the same period, mentions in his *Hymn to Apollo* that Apollo, after receiving a chariot drawn by swans from Zeus, traveled not to Delphi as instructed, but to the land of the Hyperboreans, where he remained for a year.

Ananius, a 6th century BC Ionian iambic poet, equated the Hyperboreans with the Scythians.

Simonides, a poet from Iulis in Ceos, claimed that the Hyperboreans lived for a thousand years.

Hecataeus of Miletus, known as the "Father of Geography," incorporated the Riphean Mountains in his cosmography, placing the Hyperboreans at the farthest extremity of the world. His sources likely drew from Argonautic traditions and poems like the *Arimaspea*.

Sophocles (497/6-406/5 BC) placed Boreas' home in northern Thrace near the Sarpedon rock, where Cleopatra, Boreas' daughter, was raised in her father's cave (*Antigone*, 980-987). He may have drawn on sources like Hesiod and Alcman, as he also references the northern mountains shrouded in night (*Oedipus Coloneus*, 1248).

Aeschylus (525/524-456/455 BC), considered the father of tragedy, similarly situated Boreas' home in Thrace, describing the northern winds from this region and mentioning the felicity of the Hyperboreans in his works (*Choephori*, 372-374; *Agamemnon*, 193, 651, 692, 1012, 1152-1153, 1418).

Hippocrates of Kos (460-370 BC), in the treatise *Air, Water, and Places*, part of the collection of texts attributed to him from the 5th century BC, discusses the geography of the extreme north known to the Greeks, particularly Scythia. In paragraph 19.1-2, he describes Scythia as lying under the Great Bear (Arctos) and to the south of the Riphean Mountains, from where Boreas blows. While he does not mention Hyperborea, Hippocrates seems to reject the possibility of anything living beyond the Riphean Mountains.

Hellanicus of Lesbos (480-395 BC), a prolific author in the last third of the 5th century BC, is reported by Clement of Alexandria in the 2nd century to have written that the Hyperboreans lived north of the Riphean Mountains. According to Hellanicus, they were taught justice and abstained from eating meat, consuming only wild fruits.

Damastes of Sigeum, a geographer and historian active around 400 BC, was likely younger than Herodotus and studied under Hellanicus. In a surviving fragment of his work, preserved by Stephanus of Byzantium, Damastes provided his understanding of the location of the Hyperboreans.

> "Hyperboreoi: a people. Protarchos affirms that the Alps received the name of Rhipaian Mountains, and those living beyond the Alpine mountains are all named Hyperboreoi. Antimachos says that they are identical with the Arimaspoi. But Damastes in the essay *On Nations* writes that the Issedones live beyond the Scythians and the Arimaspoi beyond them, and beyond the Arimaspoi there are the Rhipaian mountains, from which the wind of Boreas blows; and snow never abandons them. Beyond these mountains live the Hyperboreoi, until the other sea. Others report differently." (Trans. Costa)

Hellanicus of Lesbos (480-395 BC) was a prolific author in the late 5th century BC. A fragment of his work, preserved by Clement of Alexandria in the 2nd century, reports: "Hellanikos narrates that the Hyperboreans live on the far side of the Rhipaian Mountains. They are educated in justice by refraining from eating meat, but consuming fruit from trees instead. They take those who reach sixty years of age outside the city gates and do away with them."

Protarchus, a sophist writing around 392 BC, referred to the Alps as the Riphean Mountains and identified the people living to the north of the Alps as Hyperboreans. Antimachus, writing around 405 BC, disagreed with Protarchus, claiming instead that these people were Arimaspi. Both Protarchus and Antimachus had evidently equated the Alps with the legendary Riphean Mountains.

Heraclides Ponticus (390-310 BC), a philosopher and astronomer, reported in the late 4th century BC that the Hyperboreans lived above the Alps, possibly drawing from the same tradition as Protarchus and Antimachus. He also described the Gauls who sacked Rome as raiders from Hyperborea (Plutarch,

Camillus, 22.1). Additionally, Heraclides mentioned a conversation between Abaris and Pythagoras in the presence of Phalaris. This is considered historically inaccurate because it assumes it would have been before Pythagoras arrived in Italy.

Lycurgus (390-324 BC), the orator, a contemporary of Heraclides, in his speech *Against Menesaechmus*, recounts that due to a famine among the Hyperboreans, Abaris came and served Apollo. After receiving the power of prophecy from the god, Abaris traveled throughout Greece, prophesying while carrying Apollo's arrow as his emblem (F 85 Conomis).

Aristotle (384-322 BC) concurred with Aeschylus, acknowledging that the great rivers of Scythia originated in the Riphean Mountains (*Meteorologica*, 1.13.350b). In his *History of Animals* (6.35.1), written around 345/343 BC, Aristotle also referenced Hyperborea. He recounted a myth, repeated by Aelian, in which a she-wolf can only give birth during a twelve-day period each year, reflecting the twelve days it took Leto to travel from Hyperborea to Delos in the form of a wolf, while fleeing Hera's wrath.

Megasthenes (350-290 BC), a diplomat and historian, served on several embassies between 302 and 291 BC, including one sent by Seleucus I to the court of the Indian King Chandragupta, the founder of the Maurya Empire. In his writings, Megasthenes transposed the Hyperboreans to the region above the Indus and Ganges, asserting that they lived for a thousand years. In my opinion, this would place them near Tibet, Nepal and the Tarim Basin.

Simmias, writing in the early 3rd century BC, placed the rich land of the far-off Hyperboreans, where the princely Perseus once feasted, near the land of the Massagetae to the east of the Caspian Sea on the Great Steppe. He also mentioned islands in the land of the Hyperboreans.

Eratosthenes (276-195/4 BC), head of the Alexandrian library and a polymath, is noted by Strabo (1.3.22) for criticizing Herodotus' claim (4.36) that there are no Hyperboreans because there are no Hypernotians, indicating that the debate about the existence of the Hyperboreans persisted during his time.

Apollonius Rhodius in his *Argonautica*, from the 3rd century BCE, writes of a return voyage to Greece from Colchis, which would have been situated on the eastside of the Black Sea.

> "Argo sailed swiftly and entered deep into the stream of Eridanus, where Phaethon, struck by a blazing bolt, fell from the chariot of Helios into the depths of a deep lake. Even now, the lake belches up heavy clouds of steam from the smoldering wound. No bird can fly across the water; instead, they plunge into the flame and flutter. Around them, the Heliades, the daughters of Helios, enclosed in tall poplars, wail mournfully, shedding bright amber tears that fall to the ground. The sun dries these tears on the

sand, but whenever the waters of the dark lake overflow the shore under the force of a wailing wind, they roll into Eridanus in a swelling tide. The Celts say that these are the tears of Apollo, Leto's son, carried along by the eddies—countless tears he shed long ago when he visited the sacred race of the Hyperboreans, leaving the shining heavens after his father Zeus scolded him. He was angry over his son, Asclepius, born to the divine Coronis in bright Lakereia at the mouth of Amyros. Such is the story told among these people.

But the heroes felt no desire for food or drink, nor did they find any joy. They were greatly troubled all day, heavy-hearted, and faint from the unbearable stench that the streams of Eridanus emitted from the still-burning Phaethon. At night, they heard the piercing lament of the Heliades, wailing with shrill voices. As they cried, their tears floated on the water like drops of oil. From there, they entered the deep stream of Rhodanos, which flows into Eridanus, where the two rivers meet, creating a roaring mix of waters. This river, originating from the ends of the earth where the portals and homes of Nyx (Night) are located, flows in three directions: onto the shore of Oceanus, into the Ionian Sea, and through seven mouths into the Sardinian Sea and its boundless bay. From Rhodanos, they entered stormy lakes that stretched across the vast Celtic mainland, where they nearly met with disaster, as a branch of the river was carrying them toward a gulf of Oceanus."

Argonautica is an epic poem recounting the mythological tale of Jason and the Argonauts. The epic describes their quest to retrieve the Golden Fleece from Colchis. Their voyage takes them through perilous waters and lands, including the treacherous clashing rocks (Symplegades), the island of Lemnos, and the land of the Amazons. They face numerous challenges, such as the harpies tormenting the prophet Phineus and the fire-breathing bulls and dragon guarding the Golden Fleece.

After successfully acquiring the fleece with the help of Medea, the daughter of King Aeëtes of Colchis, the Argonauts encounter further difficulties on their return journey. They are driven off course, leading them through the Danube River and into the Adriatic Sea, eventually reaching the island of Circe, where they seek purification for the murder of Medea's brother.

Their journey continues through the mythical landscape of the Mediterranean and beyond, encountering various peoples and cultures, including those associated with Celtic mythology, culminating in their return to Iolcus.

From his description, likely mythical in scope, the stream of Eridanus appears to be geothermal, similar to places such as Iceland, Alaska, northeast Siberia, Italy, Yellowstone, or the boiling river of Peru. The text also describes the river with a bad stench, suggesting geothermal activity and possibly sulfuric emissions. The Celts are connected to the Hyperboreans in some way, or at least have knowledge of them. This connection emphasizes the narrative's blending of myth with real-world geography and cultures, and as such, there might not be much to be gained.

Plato's writings include a brief mention of a Hyperborean named Abaris. Herodotus also alludes to Abaris, noting that he traveled around the world without eating, carrying an arrow symbolizing his connection to Apollo. This arrow was also said to allow Abaris to fly. While Herodotus himself expresses skepticism about some of the more fantastical elements of Abaris's story, the mention of such a figure suggests that the Hyperboreans were considered a real people from a distant northern land by some ancient Greeks.

Additionally, some accounts link Abaris with the Greek philosopher Pythagoras. According to these stories, Abaris visited Greece and shared knowledge with Pythagoras, indicating a potential cross-cultural exchange of ideas. For instance, *The Oxford Companion to Philosophy* likens Pythagoras's philosophical views to those of a "Siberian shaman," suggesting an affinity with mystical practices associated with northern peoples. Plato writes:

> "If you have enough self-control, then you won't need the spells of Zalmoxis or Abaris the Hyperborean, and you can get the treatment for your mind right away. But if you still lack that virtue, we should use the incantation before the treatment."

The fact that Plato writes of a Hyperborean as an actual person suggests that Hyperboreans were not merely mythical but may have been real people who migrated from somewhere else. The poet Pindar, writing around the same time, offers additional insight into how some Ancient Greeks viewed Hyperborea, describing Perseus' journey to the fabled land:

> "Neither by ship nor on foot can you find the marvelous path to the meeting place of the Hyperboreans. Once, Perseus, the leader of his people, visited their homes and joined their feasts, finding them offering grand sacrifices of donkeys to the god. Apollo takes great pleasure in their festivals and praises, and he laughs at the proud stance of the animals. The Muse is ever present in their traditions; all around, the dances of girls, the loud chords of the lyre, and the cries of flutes swirl. They adorn their hair with golden laurel branches and celebrate with joy. No sickness or ruinous old age touches that blessed race; they live without toil or battles, free from the fear of harsh Nemesis. Breathing boldness, Perseus, the son of Danae, once joined this gathering of blessed men, guided there by Athena. He slew the Gorgon and returned with the head that brought stony death to the islanders, the head crowned with serpent hair."

In another work, *Olympian Ode 3*, Pindar recounts the founding of the Olympic Games and references the Hyperboreans:

"The Olympic Games were established long ago by Heracles, who placed the shining glory of a wreath of green olive leaves on his head. He brought these leaves from the shady streams of the Istros (the river Danube) as a symbol of Olympia's Games. Heracles persuaded the Hyperboreans, the servants of Apollo, with kind words to give him the tree for the sacred grove of Zeus. This tree would provide shade for all and crown those who performed brave deeds.

Heracles had seen his father's altars consecrated and the full moon's golden glow during the mid-month. He established the great Games and the four-yearly festival on the high banks of the sacred river Alpheus. However, the land of Pelops and the valleys around Cronus' hill had no beautiful trees, and the area was exposed to the harsh sun. This motivated him to journey to the land of Istria, where Artemis, the daughter of Leto and lover of horsemanship, welcomed him. Heracles had come from the peaks and glens of Arcadia, compelled by his father to fulfill Eurystheus' command to capture the Hind of the Golden Horns.

In his quest, he also saw the renowned land beyond the cold North Wind (Boreas), with its frozen breath, and marveled at the sight of the trees. Inspired, he resolved to plant these trees at the end of the twelve-lap course of the racing steeds."

One exotic explanation for Hyperborea, derived from Pindar's writings, suggests that one could not travel to their meeting place by foot or by ship and described the road as "marvelous." This raises the question: how exactly was it marvelous to the Ancient Greeks, or at least, to Pindar? If we consider the possibility of antigravitational technology, then perhaps the "road" to Hyperborea was not a physical path in the traditional sense but rather a transition or "crossing over" into an alternate reality. This dimension could potentially involve altered space and time, imperceptible to us in daily life but extraordinary to anyone who experienced it. In such a scenario, the road to Hyperborea could be an antigravitational field where time flows differently.

For the skeptic, this might seem like fanciful speculation especially when down to earth alternative explanations exist. However, let us entertain the notion that materials with unique molecular and atomic structures allow for quantum effects to manifest. This idea stems from Viktor Grebennikov, a Russian entomologist who claimed to have discovered antigravitational properties in the chitin of an endangered Siberian insect. If these materials could enable such effects, then perhaps a piece of wood or amber containing these insect remains, when exposed to certain sounds or chants, might be altered in a way that allows for quantum effects to emerge. This could result in a unique molecular geometry capable of influencing gravity, and thus, time.

In *Atlantis & Its Fate In The Postdiluvian World*, I speculated that Plato's orichalchum might describe a similar superconductive metamaterial. Could Pindar have firsthand knowledge of such a phenomenon? Likely not, but he may have transmitted an oral tradition recounting an experience of visiting the meeting place of the Hyperboreans through this extraordinary route, possibly via the Mystery religions of his time. This interpretation would suggest that the Hyperboreans had access to knowledge that would allow for one to enter, and perhaps live, within a time-dilated environment. In such a world, where seconds in our reality could equal hours, days or years in theirs, these beings could experience weightlessness and would move at speeds that would put them beyond our perception, and those of most cameras. However, let's assume Pindar was merely being a poet for the time being, and was inventing a story, or describing the usage of psychedelics. For a more grounded approach to Hyperborea, the historian Herodotus writes in his *Histories*:

"A poem by Aristeas, son of Kaüstrobios, a man from Prokonnesos, tells a story. Aristeas, who was said to be possessed by Apollo, visited the Issedones. Beyond them, he said, live the one-eyed Arimaspians, beyond whom are the Griffins that guard gold, and even further beyond are the Hyperboreans, whose land stretches to the sea. All these nations, except the Hyperboreans, are constantly at war with their neighbors. The Arimaspians drove the Issedones from their lands, the Issedones pushed the Scythians, and the Scythians pressured the Cimmerians, who lived by the southern sea and eventually left their homeland. Thus, Aristeas' story does not match the Scythian account of this region.

Regarding the Hyperborean people, neither the Scythians nor any other inhabitants of these lands tell us anything, except perhaps the Issedones. And, I think, even they say nothing; for if they did, then the Scythians would also have spoken of them, just as they speak of the one-eyed men. However, Hesiod mentions the Hyperboreans, and so does Homer in his poem *The Epigonoi*, if that poem is indeed Homer's work.

But the Delians have more to say about the Hyperboreans than anyone else. They claim that offerings wrapped in straw are sent from the Hyperboreans to Scythia. Once in Scythia, each nation hands them over to the next, passing them along until they reach the Adriatic Sea, which is the westernmost point of their journey. From there, they are taken south, with the people of Dodona being the first Greeks to receive them. From Dodona, the offerings go down to the Melian Gulf, and then are carried across to Euboea, where they are passed from one city to another until they arrive in Carystus. At this point, Andros is bypassed, as the Carystians take the offerings to Tenos, and the Tenians bring them to Delos. This, they say, is how these offerings reach Delos.

But on the first journey, the Hyperboreans sent two maidens with the offerings, who the Delians call Hyperoche and Laodice, along with five men from their people as an escort to ensure their safe passage. These men are now honored at Delos and are referred to as the Perpherees. However, when those they sent did not return, the Hyperboreans were displeased at the prospect of always sending people without them coming back. As a result, they decided to send the offerings wrapped in straw to their borders and instructed their neighbors to pass them along to the next country. This way, the offerings are said to eventually reach Delos. From my own knowledge, I can confirm that a similar custom exists: when the Thracian and Paeonian women make sacrifices to the Royal Artemis, they carry straw with them during the ritual.

I know that they do this. The Delian girls and boys cut their hair in honor of these Hyperborean maidens, who died at Delos. Before their marriage, the girls cut off a lock of hair and place it on the tomb, wrapped around a spindle (this tomb is located at the foot of an olive tree on the left side of the entrance to the temple of Artemis). The Delian boys similarly twist some of their hair around a green stalk and place it on the tomb. In this way, these maidens are honored by the people of Delos.

The same Delians also recount that two other virgins, Arge and Opis, arrived from the Hyperboreans before Hyperoche and Laodice, traveling through the same regions. These two came to bring tribute to Eileithyia [Artemis], fulfilling an obligation for aiding childbirth. However, Arge and Opis, they say, arrived with the gods themselves [Apollo and Artemis] and were honored by the Delians. The women collected gifts for them, invoking their names in a hymn composed by Olen of Lycia. It was from Delos that the islanders and Ionians learned to sing hymns to Opis and Arge, calling their names and gathering gifts. (Olen, who came from Lycia, also composed other ancient hymns sung at Delos.) Furthermore, it is said that when the thigh bones are burnt in sacrifice on the altar, all the ashes are placed on the burial site of Opis and Arge, behind the temple of Artemis, facing east, and closest to the dining hall of the people of Keos.

I have said enough about the Hyperboreans, and let that suffice; I will not recount the story of Abaris, who is said to have been a Hyperborean and who, while fasting, supposedly flew around the world using Apollo's arrow. But if there are people beyond the north wind (Boreas), then surely there are others beyond the south. It amuses me to see how many have drawn maps of the world, none of them accurately. They depict the world as round, as if drawn with a compass, surrounded by the river Oceanus, and with Asia and Europe of the same size. For my part, I will briefly describe the extent of the two and how they should be depicted."

Herodotus mentions the Issedones as a real people, who were the only ones that confirmed the existence of the Hyperboreans. Ancient sources place them in a region near modern-day Kazakhstan or southern Russia, potentially linked to the Saka people, who occupied this area from 800 BCE to 200 BCE. Herodotus situated the Issedones relatively close to the Tarim Basin, where mummies with distinct European features, fair skin, red hair and Scythian-style clothing were discovered. These mummies, found in present-day Xinjiang, China, are approximately 900 miles (about 1,450 kilometers) from the traditional territory associated with the Issedones.

The Tarim Basin, although not geographically northern, might be considered as a possible location for the source of the Hyperborean legend due to its relatively temperate climate between 1200 BCE and 400 BCE. During this period, the region experienced more rainfall, supporting forests and grasslands, which would align with descriptions of a peaceful and fertile land. The absence of fortified settlements further suggests a society that lived in relative tranquility, matching some of the characteristics ascribed to Hyperborea in ancient texts. The Tarim River, while not as large as the Nile or the Mississippi, was significantly more extensive between 4,000 BCE and 400 BCE than it is today, and likely syncs up much better with the description of a river with poplar trees than the

Lena River and others. Additionally, nearby mountain ranges, such as the Altai and Tian Shan or even the Himalayas, could be mythologically linked to the legendary Riphean Mountains mentioned in ancient texts. The Tarim Mummies represent a unique population with a substantial portion of their genetic makeup originating from the Ancient North Eurasians (ANE). Studies suggest that a significant majority of their DNA is derived from this ancient lineage. This is likely the same ancestry found in the Mandan Indians before Smallpox killed most of them. The Mandan tribe was believed to be of European descent with features such as fair skin, blonde hair and blue eyes, and who Thomas Jefferson tasked Lewis & Clark to find due to rumors of "Welsh Indians".

Based on Herodotus' accounts and other historical data, other potential locations for Hyperborea might include regions associated with the ancestors of the Tarim Mummies. These areas provide a plausible setting for the Hyperborean mythos. If one assumes that they had an oral history of their northern origins, or in a further, northeast location in the remote past, that could explain later confusion about their location, as subsequent generations may have settled further south, such as in the Tarim Basin. Another possibility is that their close proximity to the Himalayas, might have caused errors by associating the frigid cold and snow of the mountains there as the "far north". This migration and adaptation to new environments might have contributed to the diverse accounts of Hyperborea's geographical and cultural landscape, at least, if we follow Herodotus. However, one item that does not align with the Tarim Basin's known natural resources is the description of amber. According to ancient sources, amber was a significant element associated with the mythical land of Hyperborea. These sources describe the material as a product of the region, linked to various myths such as the tears of the Heliades turning into amber.

After Herodotus, the next entry we have concerning the Hyperboreans is from **Hecataeus of Abdera**, a student of the skeptic Pyrrho. Although his works, including *On Egypt* and *On the Hyperboreans*, have been lost, fragments survive through later authors such as **Diodorus Siculus**. Diodorus, in his *Bibliotheca historica*, provides a detailed description based on Hecataeus's account:

> "Since we have decided to mention the regions of Asia that lie to the north, we think it appropriate to also discuss the legendary accounts of the Hyperboreans. According to ancient myths, as told by Hecataeus and some others, there is an island in the Ocean beyond the land of the Celts, no smaller than Sicily. This island, the story goes, is located in the north and is inhabited by the Hyperboreans, who are named so because their home is beyond the place where the north wind (Boreas) blows. The island is fertile and productive, with an unusually temperate climate, allowing for two harvests each year.
>
> Moreover, the following legend is associated with it: Leto was born on this island, and for that reason, Apollo is honored above all other gods. The inhabitants are considered priests of Apollo in a way, as they praise this god daily with continuous songs and honor him greatly. The island also features a magnificent sacred precinct of Apollo and a notable temple, adorned with many votive offerings, and is spherical in shape. Additionally, there is a city on the island dedicated to this god, where most of the inhabitants are cithara players. They continually play this instrument in the temple and sing hymns of praise to the god, glorifying his deeds.
>
> The Hyperboreans are also said to have their own unique language and are very friendly towards the Greeks, especially the Athenians and the Delians, who have inherited this goodwill from ancient times. The myth also mentions that certain Greeks visited the Hyperboreans and left behind valuable votive offerings with inscriptions in Greek letters. Similarly, Abaris, a Hyperborean, came to Greece in ancient times and reaffirmed the goodwill and kinship between his people and the Delians.
>
> It is also said that from this island, the moon appears to be very close to the earth, and its surface features, such as mountains, are visible to the naked eye. Additionally, the account states that the god visits the island every nineteen years, coinciding with the period when the stars return to the same position in the heavens, which the Greeks call the 'year of Meton.' During this visit, the god plays the cithara and dances throughout the night from the vernal equinox until the rising of the Pleiades, expressing his joy in his achievements. The rulers of this city are called Boreadae, as they are descendants of Boreas (the North Wind), and the leadership positions are always kept within this family."

Based on the above description, we have been given a picture of an island around the size of Sicily,

featuring a circular temple that was associated with music and chanting. Some interpret this as a description of Stonehenge and the activities that took place there. However, England, being much larger than Sicily, doesn't fit the criteria even with ancient geography not being a precise art. Alternatively, the Isle of Man, the Orkney Islands, or even Ireland might be possible locations as Ireland was believed to be much smaller back then. One could also look north. In ancient times, Sicily was known to be around 10,000 square miles in size. Comparatively, Spitsbergen in Norway covers about 15,051 square miles. Yuzhny Island off the Russian coast is around 12,836 square miles. Other islands worth exploring are the Isle of Lewis, Faroe Islands, Gotland and Kolguyev Island. Another intriguing possibility is suggested by the description of the moon appearing differently. This could also imply that the ceremony altered gravity or time in a way that bends light, as if through a lens. Most scholars would attribute that description to mythical hearsay or the usage of psychedelics, however.

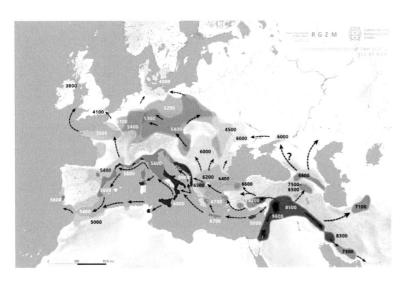

Of particular interest is that the builders of Stonehenge were likely descended from the Early European Farmers (EEF), who began spreading across Europe around 9,600 BCE. This timing coincides with Plato's suggested date for the destruction of Atlantis, a period also marked by numerous myths and legends of survivors from a great flood arriving in the very area where this group emerges. Notably, this era aligns with the submergence of Beringia into the ocean and a series of cataclysmic events in North and South America that led to the extinction of 80% of large mammal species and which also killed or displaced the vast majority of people living in North America at that time.

Around 7,000 BCE, a group of these Early European Farmers migrated around the Caspian Sea, in the direction of Siberia, the Tarim Basin and Tibet. Other groups migrated westward, reaching Malta, where they left behind megalithic monuments, an underground temple and elongated skulls as mentioned in the preface. By approximately 4,100 BCE, these people arrived in the British Isles, reaching Ireland around 3,800 BCE. Those EEF settlers are credited with constructing monumental structures like Stonehenge.

Noteworthy sites that may correspond to these ancient cultural practices include the Meayll Circle on the Isle of Man, Newgrange in Ireland, and Maeshowe on the Orkney Islands. However, much like the Hypogeum in Malta which will be discussed later, it is quite possible other sites exist that remain undiscovered on both these and other islands.

Although many contemporary scholars consider the cultures that built monuments such as Stonehenge as primitive, the Gaelic myths of the **Tuatha de Danann**—a legendary race in Irish mythology—suggest otherwise. These myths, likely passed down to Celtic invaders who arrived with the Indo-European migrations around 500-1000 BCE, describe fantastical elements such as flying ships, destructive weapons, the ability to stop time, and even a mechanical arm covered with synthetic flesh. Additionally, the Tuatha de Danann were reputed to possess knowledge of necromancy or the ability to resurrect the dead.

It is worth exploring the possibility that the Early European Farmers, who likely were responsible for sites

like Stonehenge, Silbury Hill, Newgrange, and the Hal Saflieni Hypogeum on Malta, might have been connected to the group that was responsible for the legends of the **Tuatha de Danann**, and that this group could have possessed advanced knowledge and practices, possibly passed down from a lost civilization. While modern scholarship often disputes these connections, mainly suggesting genetic links due to migration, a theory proposed in Chapter 2 explores the possibility that, based on descriptions of Abaris the Hyperborean and the claims of Viktor Grebennikov—who reportedly built a flying machine from the chitin of an insect species in Siberia—this group might have possessed advanced capabilities, such as flight and the ability to reverse biological aging. This could explain their presence in distant locations, such as the Tarim Basin, Ancient Greece, Malta, the British Isles, and even unique finds like the mini-Stonehenge discovered in Lake Michigan under Traverse Bay (shown in the photos on this page), dating before 7,000 BCE, as well as the elongated skulls found in the Americas.

Diodorus continues in his **Library of History 3.59.6:**

> "In Phrygian mythology, they say that Apollo placed both the lyre and
> the pipes as offerings in the cave of Dionysus. Afterward, he became infatuated with Cybele and
> accompanied her on her journeys all the way to the land of the Hyperboreans."

Diodorus Siculus, Library of History 4.51.1-4:

"Medea, while living with Jason in the Thessalian kingdom of Pelias, disguised herself as a priestess of Artemis from Hyperborea. She created a hollow statue of Artemis, hiding various drugs inside it. She also applied potent ointments to her hair, turning it grey, and made her face and body appear wrinkled, so that everyone who saw her believed she was an old woman.

At dawn, carrying the statue of the goddess designed to terrify the superstitious people and incite their fear of the gods, Medea entered the city. Acting as if she were inspired, she gathered the crowd along the streets and called on everyone to welcome the goddess with reverence. She told them that the goddess had come from the Hyperboreans to bring good fortune to the entire city and the king. While all the inhabitants worshiped the goddess and honored her with sacrifices, and the whole city, along with Medea herself, behaved as if they were inspired, she made her way into the palace.

Medea proclaimed that Artemis, riding through the air in a chariot drawn by dragon-serpents, had flown over many parts of the inhabited world and had chosen the realm of the most devout king as the place to establish her worship and receive eternal honors."

NOTE: A recurring theme in reported extraterrestrial encounters is that witnesses often experience overwhelming fear, sometimes resulting in paralysis. An illustrative example is from Skinwalker Ranch, where two men walking through the area reported encountering a being in a tree. Upon making eye contact with this entity, they were suddenly gripped by an intense sense of terror. This phenomenon could, however, be explained by a technological mechanism—perhaps a method that was used in the distant past to control human beings much in the way dogs are controlled by high frequencies in the ultrasonic range—but which affects the fear centers in the human brain, inducing a state of paralysis. Infrasound, characterized by sound waves below 20 Hz, has been linked to inducing fear and discomfort in humans. Often called the "fear frequency," around 19 Hz, these low-frequency vibrations are usually imperceptible to the ear but can cause a visceral sense of unease and terror. The subtle, almost subliminal nature of infrasound can manifest as physical sensations like nausea and headaches, as well as psychological effects, including anxiety and a sense of dread. This phenomenon has been noted in various experiments, where exposure to infrasound led participants to experience an eerie or ominous atmosphere, even in the absence of any overt threat.

The implications of this might suggest that ancient technologies harnessed certain frequencies as a means of psychological influence or control. Just as modern ultrasonic devices create invisible boundaries for animals, infrasound could have been used to manipulate human emotions and perceptions, inducing fear and controlling behavior.

Descriptions in Ancient Greek myth such as those above, and Medusa turning any that looked at her into stone, could be a memory of the effect those wielding such technology had on others. In addition, the association with dragon serpents and flight, while visually compelling as myth, should also be considered as a potential metaphor for the spiral motifs prevalent in prehistoric art. This symbolism might hint at advanced technological concepts, such as the idea that rotating certain materials at specific speeds could generate quantum effects, including antigravity. This concept is supported by experiments conducted by Dr. Ning Li and Eugene Podkletnov, who explored the potential of antigravity through the rotation of superconducting discs and the manipulation of gravitomagnetic fields.

Dr. Ning Li, alongside Douglas Torr, proposed that rotating ions could generate a gravitomagnetic field, potentially leading to a repulsive force capable of reducing the weight of objects. This was demonstrated in her work on superconductors, which suggested that under certain conditions, significant weight reduction could occur. Similarly, Eugene Podkletnov claimed to observe a weight reduction effect in objects placed above a rotating disc, describing a "gravity shielding" phenomenon that could reduce an object's weight by up to 2%. Interestingly, tornadoes, which are characterized by rapidly rotating vortices of air, have often been described as producing a sound similar to the buzzing of bees, who also create similar vortices in the air with their wings. This description highlights the distinctive, continuous hum or drone associated with the high-speed rotation of air and debris within the tornado's funnel. The sound can vary depending on the tornado's intensity, the landscape it traverses, and the objects it picks up, but the comparison to buzzing is a common observation made by those who have experienced or studied tornadoes. We'll delve deeper into quantum geometry and its potential implications for antigravity at a later time.

Aeschylus, an eminent Greek tragedian from the 5th century B.C., briefly mentions the Hyperboreans in his play *Libation Bearers*. The line reflects the perception of Hyperborea as an idealized land:

> "Your wish is better than gold. It surpasses great good fortune, even that of the Hyperboreans."

Pseudo-Apollodorus, a Greek mythographer from the 2nd century A.D., compiled the *Bibliotheca*, a comprehensive summary of Greek myths and legends. He recounts several tales involving the Hyperboreans:

> "Artemis shot him, the giant Orion, as he was forcing his advances on Opis, a virgin who had come from the Hyperboreans."

> "[The golden apples of the Hesperides:] These apples were not, as some say, in Libya, but rather were with Atlas among the Hyperboreans. Gaia (the Earth) had given them to Zeus when he married Hera."

NOTE: The golden apples of the Hesperides, noted for bestowing immortality and eternal youth, bear similarities to the legends of the Holy Grail and the Philosopher's Stone. While the Holy Grail is often depicted as a chalice, some traditions describe it as a red stone, akin to the Philosopher's Stone, which was believed to grant immortality and transmute base metals into gold. Plato's reference to orichalcum, a metal from Atlantis that was said to no longer exist in Plato's time, was also said to gleam with a red light. The Fountain of Youth is another legend with a similar theme of immortality, describing it as a water source that bestows eternal youth on those who drink from it. The Greeks also had the myth of the "Nectar and Ambrosia," the divine drink and food consumed by the gods on Mount Olympus. These substances were believed to grant immortality and eternal youth to the gods, preventing them from aging or dying. Mortals who consumed nectar or ambrosia, according to myths, could also gain similar divine attributes, reinforcing the idea that consuming certain mystical substances could grant everlasting life. Ancient myths, like those from Herodotus, spoke of a spring in Aethiopia with rejuvenating properties, which is where the legend of the Fountain of Youth began. Interestingly, Homer and other ancient historians, such as Ephorus and Philostratus, placed Aethiopia's origins in the east rather than the south, suggesting a different geographical perspective than is commonly accepted today. According to the ancient historical accounts, some believed that the Aethiopians migrated from regions near India, close to the Tarim Basin, where the famous Tarim mummies were discovered. Furthermore, the discovery of *Diospyros ebenum* wood from Sri Lanka or southern India in Egyptian artifacts from the 5th Dynasty has led some to speculate that the Egyptian land of Punt, often considered the "*Land of the Gods*," might have been located in Sri Lanka instead of around Somalia, as commonly thought. While no definitive evidence of early civilization has been found in Sri Lanka, records suggest that the earliest inhabitants engaged in a form of serpent worship. The Naga people are believed to have been an ancient tribe inhabiting Sri Lanka and various regions of Southern India. They are frequently mentioned in ancient texts such as the *Mahavamsa*, *Manimekalai*, *Mahabharata*, and other Sanskrit and Pali literature. In these sources, the Nagas are often depicted as a class of superhuman beings who could take the form of serpents. They were thought to inhabit a mystical, subterranean realm. It's worth considering if the description of taking the form of a serpent might refer to how they dressed, particularly in shamanic rituals, where costumes and symbolic attire could be used to embody spiritual entities.

In another text, Diodorus Siculus describes the Amazons as wearing armor made from the skin of a serpent that they wore for defensive purposes. This could relate to historical practices of using tough animal skins for protection. For instance, the **Calabar Burrowing Python** (Calabaria reinhardtii) is known for having exceptionally thick and tough skin. Its skin is up to 15 times thicker than that of other snakes and has a highly organized structure, making it resistant to punctures and abrasions.

Given the durability of such skin, it is plausible that ancient peoples, including those possibly identified as Nagas, might have used the skin of tough-skinned snakes similar to the Calabar Burrowing Python as armor. This use of snake skin could have led to legends and descriptions of people transforming into serpents, symbolically representing their protective gear or attire. Such armor would not only serve a practical defensive function but also carry symbolic and ritualistic significance, aligning with the mythological portrayal of the Nagas as powerful, otherworldly beings.

"Prometheus advised Heracles not to go after the apples of the Hesperides himself, but instead to relieve Atlas of holding up the sky and send him to retrieve them. So when Heracles reached Atlas among the Hyperboreans, he remembered Prometheus' advice and took over holding the celestial sphere. Atlas then picked three apples from the garden of the Hesperides and returned to Heracles."

NOTE: The exact location of the Hesperides' garden was a subject of mythological ambiguity, but it was generally believed to be situated at the westernmost edge of the known world. According to ancient Greek cosmology, this placed it near the boundary of the world and the Oceanus, the vast river believed to encircle the earth. Some sources suggest the garden was associated with regions beyond the Pillars of Heracles (modern-day Strait of Gibraltar), in what was considered the far west.

Apollonius Rhodius, a Greek epic poet from the 3rd century B.C., is known for his epic poem *Argonautica*. He writes about the Hyperboreans and their connection to the god Apollo:

"And to them, Apollo, the son of Leto, appeared as he traveled from Lycia far away to the countless people of the Hyperboreans; his golden locks flowed in clusters on both sides of his cheeks as he moved."

NOTE: Lycia was an ancient region located in the southwestern part of Anatolia, present-day Turkey, along the Mediterranean coast. It lay between Caria to the west and Pamphylia to the east, with the Taurus Mountains forming its northern boundary. Lycia had a unique cultural and political structure, including the Lycian League, which was a federation of city-states with a form of representative democracy that influenced later political thought, including aspects of the United States Constitution.

Lycia's history dates back to the Late Bronze Age, and it was mentioned in Hittite and Egyptian records as part of the Sea Peoples' confederation. Throughout its history, Lycia was often caught between larger powers, such as the Persian Empire and later the Roman Empire. Despite these influences, the Lycians maintained a distinct identity. The region is noted for its rock-cut tombs, especially those in the cities of Xanthos and Myra, which display a unique blend of Greek and Persian architectural styles

Callimachus, a notable Greek poet and scholar from the 3rd century B.C., is known for his hymns and elegies. In *Hymn 4 to Delos*, he describes the offerings from the Hyperboreans:

"You [Delos] are renowned as the most sacred of islands, the nurturer of Apollo's youth. Neither Enyo, nor Hades, nor the horses of Ares tread upon you; instead, every year, tithes of first-fruits are sent to you. Choirs come to you from all cities, from those in the East, the West, the South, **and even from the Hyperboreans—a very long-lived race who live above the northern shore.** The Hyperboreans are the first to bring you cornstalks and holy sheaves of corn-ears, which are received by the Pelasgians of Dodona [the famous oracle of Zeus] as these offerings enter their land from afar. Next, the offerings come to the sacred town and mountains of the Malian land; from there, they are carried across to the fertile Lelantian plain of the Abantes [the island of Euboea]. And the voyage from Euboea to your havens is not long, for they are close by.

The first to bring these offerings from the fair-haired Arimaspians were Opis and Loxo and the blessed Hecaerge, daughters of Boreas (the North Wind), along with the best of the young men of that time. These bearers did not return home, but they met a fortunate fate and will never lose their glory. Indeed, the girls of Delos, when the sweet-sounding marriage hymn reaches the maidens' quarters, offer their maiden hair as a tribute to these maidens, while the boys present the first growth of the down on their cheeks to the young men."

In his *Fragments*, Callimachus briefly notes the peculiar offerings of the Hyperboreans:

"Phoebus [Apollo] visits the sacrifices of asses offered by the Hyperboreans."

"Fat sacrifices of asses please Phoebus [Apollo]."

"They [the Hyperboreans] send offerings [to Apollo at Delos] from the Rhipaean Mountains."

NOTE: From the above, a site which features the mass bones of donkeys, suggesting ritual sacrifice, may provide clues to its actual location. The Tarim Basin, Altai region, and the British Isles/Ireland are all significant regions associated with early agricultural practices, particularly the cultivation of wheat and barley.

In ancient European contexts, "corn" referred to these grains, rather than maize. The Tarim Basin's involvement in early wheat and barley cultivation aligns it with descriptions of "cornstalks and holy sheaves of corn-ears." However, all are plausible candidates for producing the grains described in historical texts, fitting the accounts of offerings made by the Hyperboreans.

His description *"above the northern shore,"* likely suggests the British Isles or some other island north of Europe or Asia, however.

Strabo, a Greek geographer and historian from the late 1st century B.C. to the early 1st century A.D., compiled *Geography*, an important source of ancient geographical knowledge. He critiques the mythical accounts of the Hyperboreans:

"It is due to people's ignorance of these regions [i.e., the land of the Thracian Getae, now Bulgaria and Romania] that any attention has been paid to those who invented the mythical 'Rhipaean Mountains and Hyperborea,' as well as to the false statements made by Pytheas of Massalia [a Greek writer from the 4th century BCE] regarding the lands along the Oceanus, where he hides behind his scientific knowledge of astronomy and mathematics. Therefore, those men should be disregarded. In fact, even Sophocles [the tragedian from the 5th century BCE], in his role as a tragic poet, speaks of Oreithyia, telling how she was snatched up by Boreas (the North Wind) and carried 'over the entire sea to the ends of the earth, to the sources of night, and to [Hyperborea], the ancient garden of Phoebus [Apollo].'"

Pausanias, a Greek traveler and geographer from the 2nd century A.D., authored *Description of Greece*, a valuable guide to ancient Greek landmarks and their associated myths. He provides several references to the Hyperboreans:

Pausanias, *Description of Greece* 1.18.5:

"In Athens, there is a temple dedicated to Eileithyia, who, according to legend, came from the Hyperboreans to Delos and assisted Leto during her labor; from Delos, the worship of Eileithyia spread to other peoples. The Delians offer sacrifices to Eileithyia and sing a hymn by Olen [a legendary poet]. Among the Athenians, the wooden figures of Eileithyia are draped to the feet. The oldest of these figures was brought from Delos by Erysichthon."

NOTE: While specific details about these garments are scarce, the description of the wooden figures of Eileithyia being fully clothed in woven fabric suggests a high level of textile craftsmanship, similar to that seen in the clothing of a Tarim mummy as shown in the photo here to the right.

Pausanias, *Description of Greece* 1.31.2:

"At Prasiai [a village near Athens], there is a temple of Apollo. It is said that the first-fruits from the Hyperboreans are sent here. The Hyperboreans are believed to pass them to the Arimaspians, who then pass them to the Issedones. The Issedones give them to the Scythians, who bring them to Sinope. From there, Greeks transport them to Prasiai, and the Athenians carry them to Delos. The first-fruits are hidden in wheat straw, and their contents are unknown to all. At Prasiai, there is also a monument to Erysichthon, who died on the journey back from Delos after the sacred mission there."

NOTE: The Tarim Basin was a significant agricultural region in ancient Central Asia, known for the cultivation of wheat and barley. Archaeological evidence from key sites like Wupaer and Xiaohe reveals that wheat was a staple crop, essential to the region's subsistence. The introduction and development of wheat cultivation in the Tarim Basin can be traced back several millennia, with substantial agricultural advancements occurring between 1500 and 400 BCE. Interestingly, Tibet, lying just south of the Tarim

Basin, offers a geographical source for the ancient concept of the Riphean Mountains. The Himalayas, with

their towering, snow-capped peaks and frigid environments, might have been the true source of this legend. Ancient historians may have misinterpreted reports of the cold, mountainous environment of the Himalayas as being in the far north, and mislocated that mountain range. Alternatively, the legend itself could have originated south of the Himalayas from India or the Levant in the distant past, carried along ancient trade routes and evolving as it traveled due to an incomplete geographic picture of the world.

Pausanias, *Description of Greece* 3.13.2:

"The Lacedaemonians [of Sparta] have a temple dedicated to the Saviour Maid [Artemis]. Some say it was constructed by Orpheus the Thracian, while others attribute it to Abaris when he came from the Hyperboreans."

Pausanias, *Description of Greece* 5.7.6-9:

"Regarding the Olympic games, the most knowledgeable antiquarians of Elis say that Cronus was the first king of heaven and that a temple was built in his honor at Olympia by the people of that era, who were called the Golden Race. When Zeus was born, Rhea entrusted the care of her son to the Dactyls of Ida. These Dactyls came from Cretan Ida and were named Heracles, Paeonaeus, Epimedes, Iasius, and Idas. Heracles, being the eldest, organized a running race among his brothers as a game, and crowned the winner with a branch of wild olive. They had such an abundance of olive branches that they slept on piles of the leaves while they were still green. **It is said that the wild olive was introduced into Greece by Heracles from the land of the Hyperboreans, people living beyond the home of Boreas (the North Wind).**

Olen the Lycian, in his hymn to Achaea, was the first to say that Achaea came to Delos from these Hyperboreans. Later, Melanopus of Cyme composed an ode to Opis and Hecaerge, stating that they, even before Achaea, came to Delos from the Hyperboreans.

Aristeas of Proconnesus, who also mentioned the Hyperboreans, **might have learned more about them from the Issedones**, as he mentions in his poem that he visited them."

"[On the founding of the Delphic Oracle:] Boeo, a native woman who composed a hymn for the Delphians, said that the oracle was established for the god Apollo by visitors from the Hyperboreans, including Olen [a semi-legendary poet] and others. Olen was the first to prophesy and chant the hexameter oracles. The verses of Boeo are as follows: 'Here in truth, a mindful oracle was built by the sons of the Hyperboreans, Pagasos and divine Agyieos.' After naming other Hyperboreans, she concludes the hymn with Olen: 'And Olen, who became the first prophet of Phoebus, and first composed a song of ancient verses.' However, tradition does not mention any other male prophet, only prophetesses.

It is said that the oldest temple of Apollo was made from laurel, with branches brought from the laurel in Tempe. This temple likely resembled a hut. The Delphians claim that the second temple was made by bees from beeswax and feathers and that Apollo sent it to the Hyperboreans."

"[When the Gauls invaded Greece in 279 B.C.:] South of the Gates [of Thermopylae], they showed little interest in capturing other towns, focusing instead on sacking Delphi and the treasures of the god [Apollo]. They were opposed by the Delphians, the Phocians from the cities around Mount Parnassus, and a force of Aetolians, who were known for their vigor at the time. During the battle, not only were thunderbolts and rocks hurled at the Gauls from Parnassus, but also terrifying shapes resembling armed warriors appeared to haunt the foreigners. It is said that two of these figures, Hyperochus and Amadocus, came from the Hyperboreans, and the third was Pyrrhus, son of Achilles."

NOTE: The reference to the introduction of the wild olive from Hyperborea by Heracles suggests a connection between Hyperborea and regions that might have had wild olive trees. The wild olive tree is generally only found in the Mediterranean, Asia Minor and North Africa. Considerations of the climate in other areas 2,500 to 4,000 years ago, along with finds of wild olive trees in those regions, could point to a potential marker for Hyperborea. The mention of the Issedones would seem to suggest, much like Herodotus, that they would be in that general area associated with the Tarim Basin or north of the Caspian Sea; which conflicts with the claim of the wild olive tree, unless, it originally came from a region further east or northeast when climatic conditions were different.

Also of note is the description of the influence the Hyperboreans had on the development of the Oracle at Delphi, suggesting they chanted in hexameter, and that one of the temples consisted of beeswax and feathers. The preternatural description of them fighting the Celts could suggest advanced technology, involving electricity and antigravitational abilities as well as perhaps a psychotropic weapon, similar to that discussed earlier regarding infrasound's effect on human perception. These descriptions may also provide some additional hints on the culture of the Hyperboreans as related to oracles, prophesying and their connections to Delos, which will be covered in more detail in Chapters 2 and 3. The legends of the Tuatha de Danann, also include a legend of traveling from Ireland to Greece, where they were enslaved for a period of time, before they returned.

It should also be noted that Pausanias, in describing another local legend, also places the introduction of the wild olive to Greece, near the Saronic Sea.

Antoninus Liberalis, a Greek mythographer from the 2nd century A.D., wrote *Metamorphoses*, a collection of transformation myths. He includes a story involving the Hyperboreans:

> "Apollo and Artemis had a great affection for him [the Babylonian man Clinis], and he often accompanied these gods to the temple of Apollo in the land of the Hyperboreans, where he witnessed the consecration of the sacrifices of asses to the god. Upon returning to Babylon, he desired to worship the god in the same manner as the Hyperboreans and prepared a hecatomb of asses by the altar. Apollo appeared and threatened him with death if he did not stop this sacrifice and instead offer the usual goats, sheep, and cattle. The sacrifice of asses was pleasing to the god only when performed by the Hyperboreans."

NOTE: This may suggest a location closer to Babylon, which was located just south of modern day Baghdad, between the years 2300 to 539 BCE. Clinis is a mythological figure, for which little is known, and it is possible the Babylonian description could apply to Sumer, which would hypothetically place the dates as far back as 4500 BCE.

Pomponius Mela, the earliest Roman geographer, wrote the geographical essay *De Chorographia* during the reigns of Gaius and Claudius (37-41 AD). Drawing from previous authors, particularly Herodotus, he placed the Hyperboreans beyond the Sea of Azov on the Asian coast, under the North Pole, beyond the North Wind, and the Riphean Mountains (1.116-2.1, 3.5.36).

Ptolemy (100-170 AD), a Roman mathematician and geographer, did not dispute the existence of the Hyperboreans or the Riphean Mountains. Following Aristeas' ideas as presented in Herodotus (4.13), he located the Riphean Mountains in the middle of the Russian Steppe (3.5.5) and mentioned a sacred isle and a Hyperborean Ocean to the north.

Maximus of Tyre, a rhetorician and philosopher from the late 2nd century, recounted how Aristeas' soul could leave his body, traverse sea and land, and reach the Hyperboreans (38:3).

In the 3rd century, **Priscian** (307, 570-575 AD) wrote that the Riphean Mountains were located to the north of the Black Sea. However, taking Pindar into account, he suggested that the Hyperboreans had, in earlier times, been neighbors of the Ethiopians. It should be noted again that Homer had placed Ethiopia to the east, not to the south, and two other ancient historians wrote that the Ethiopians came from India or the Far East. Ancient sources also spoke of *white ethiopians*. The word for Ethiopia in Ancient Greek means *"burnt face"*.

Aelian, a Greek author known for his works on natural history, wrote *On Animals* in the late 2nd and early 3rd centuries A.D. He includes a reference to the Hyperboreans:

    Aelian, *On Animals* 4.4:

"Wolves have a difficult time giving birth, usually taking twelve days and twelve nights. The people of Delos believe this is the same amount of time it took for Leto to travel from the Hyperboreans to Delos."

Aelian, *On Animals* 11.1:

"The race of the Hyperboreans and the honors they pay to Apollo are well-known, being celebrated by both poets and historians, including Hecataeus, not from Miletus but from Abdera [a Greek philosopher from the 4th century BCE]. This god [Apollo] has priests who are the sons of Boreas (the North Wind) and Chione (Snow), three brothers by birth, each six cubits tall. At the appointed time, when they perform the customary rituals for the aforementioned god, swans descend from what are called the Rhipaean mountains. These swans arrive in great numbers, flying around the temple as if purifying it with their flight. They then settle in the temple precinct, an area of immense size and exceptional beauty.

Whenever the singers begin their hymns to the god, accompanied by harpers with harmonious music, the swans join in the song in perfect harmony. They never sing a discordant note or go out of tune, as if they were guided by a conductor, harmonizing perfectly with the natives who are skilled in the sacred melodies. When the hymn ends, these winged choristers, as they might be called, after fulfilling their customary service and praising the god throughout the day, depart."

Aelian, *On Animals* 11.10:

"I have mentioned the swans from the Rhipaean Mountains in the land of the Hyperboreans because of their daily and devoted service to Apollo, the son of Zeus and Leto."

Aelian, *Historical Miscellany* 2.26:

"Aristotle says that Pythagoras [6th century BCE] was referred to by the citizens of Crotus as Apollo Hyperboreus (Apollo of the Hyperboreans)."

NOTE: Aelian mentions that the Hyperboreans were six cubits tall, which is up to nine feet in height. His description of a 12 day journey would indicate a location very close to Greece, unless, as discussed in a later chapter, flight was involved. Most importantly, Pythagoras was associated by name with the Hyperboreans.

Philostratus the Elder, a Greek rhetorician from the 3rd century A.D., in his work *Imagines*, describes a mythical story related to the Hyperboreans:

"Golden are the tears of the daughters of Helios (the Sun). The story goes that they shed these tears for Phaëthon, who, in his desire to drive, dared to take his father's chariot. However, because he couldn't control the horses, he met with disaster and fell into the river Eridanus...The youth was thrown from the chariot and fell headlong—his hair ablaze and his chest smoldering from the heat. His fall ended in the river Eridanus, giving the river a legendary tale.

Swans scattered around, singing sweet notes, will sing about the youth; and flocks of swans rising into the air will carry the tale to the rivers Cayster and Ister [rivers of Lycia and Scythia]. No place will remain unaware of the strange story. They will be accompanied by Zephyros (the West Wind), the swift god of the wayside shrines, who is said to have made an agreement with the swans to join them in the music of the lament. This agreement is already being fulfilled, for look! The wind is playing upon the swans as if they were musical instruments."

NOTE: Swans were present in all of the regions mentioned, including the Tarim Basin when its climatic conditions were less dry and arid. Species of swans that might fit the description include the **Whooper Swan** (*Cygnus cygnus*) and the **Mute Swan** (*Cygnus olor*), both of which are common to the region. Swans are also famously present in other parts of the world, such as **Northern Europe** (especially in countries like the UK, Scandinavia, and Russia), **North America** (where species like the **Trumpeter Swan** and **Tundra Swan** are found), and **Australia** (home to the unique **Black Swan**). It is also possible that the swan imagery serves as a symbolic or metaphorical reference, potentially describing technological instruments or something else entirely, a theory that will be explored in a later chapter.

Pseudo-Hyginus, a Roman mythographer from the 2nd century A.D., in his work *Astronomica*, recounts a myth involving the Hyperboreans:

> **Pseudo-Hyginus, *Astronomica* 2.15 (trans. Grant):**
>
> "Eratosthenes [a Greek writer from the 3rd century B.C.] says about the Arrow, that with this Apollo killed the Cyclops who had forged the thunderbolt by which Aesculapius [Asclepius] died. Apollo had buried this arrow in the Hyperborean mountain, but when Jupiter [Zeus] pardoned his son, it was carried by the wind and returned to Apollo along with the grain that was growing at that time. Many believe that this is why it is among the constellations."

NOTE: The "arrow in the Hyperborean mountain" likely refers to the legend of Abaris, who was said to ride on Apollo's arrow across the world.

Clement of Alexandria, an early Christian theologian from the 2nd to 3rd centuries A.D., wrote *Exhortation to the Greeks*, where he criticized the pagan temples and mentioned the Hyperboreans:

> "These temples [those of the pagan Greeks] are referred to by a pleasant-sounding name, but in truth, they are tombs. I urge you, even now, to abandon the worship of demons,

feeling ashamed to honor tombs...Why should I mention the Hyperborean women? They are known as Hyperoche and Laodice, and they rest in the Artemision (Temple of Artemis) at Delos; this is within the temple precincts of Delian Apollo."

NOTE: This may imply an association with the Hyperboreans with occult practices and witchcraft, and an association with the temples at Delos with Hyperborean architecture.

Ovid, a Roman poet from the 1st century B.C. to the 1st century A.D., in his epic work *Metamorphoses*, recounts various mythical transformations and tales, including a story about the Hyperboreans:

Ovid, *Metamorphoses* 10.352 ff:

"If some black bitumen catches fire or yellow sulfur burns with little smoke, then surely, when the ground no longer provides such fuel and oily nourishment for flames...It is said that the Hyperboreans of Pallene can cover their entire bodies with light feathers by plunging nine times in Minerva's [Athena's] marsh [i.e., a lake of bitumen]. But I cannot believe another tale: that Scythian women achieve a similar transformation by having poison sprinkled on their limbs."

NOTE: Pallene is usually associated with the Gigantomachy, the mythic battle between the gods and the giants, and it is a region in ancient Greece, specifically one of the three peninsulas of the Chalcidice. According to myth, the Giants were born from the blood of Uranus, the sky god, when he was castrated by his son Cronus. As the blood spilled onto Gaia, the Earth, she gave birth to the Giants. These beings were enormous and powerful, often depicted with human-like upper bodies and serpentine lower bodies, embodying the primal forces of chaos and nature.

Gaia, angered by the imprisonment of the Titans—her other children—in Tartarus, incited the Giants to rebel against the Olympian gods. The Giants sought to overthrow the gods and claim dominion over the cosmos, leading to a cataclysmic conflict known as the Gigantomachy.

The battle between the Giants and the Olympians was a prolonged war. The Giants launched an assault on Mount Olympus, hurling huge boulders and flaming trees as weapons. The Olympians, led by Zeus, fought back with all their might. Each god played a specific role in the battle: Zeus wielded his thunderbolts, Athena used her wisdom and combat skills, and Apollo and Artemis fought with their archery skills. A crucial prophecy foretold that the gods could not defeat the Giants without the aid of a mortal. Hercules (Heracles), fulfilling this prophecy, joined the battle. His arrows, dipped in the poisonous blood of the Hydra, were instrumental in slaying many of the Giants.

Ultimately, the Olympians triumphed, defeating the Giants and restoring order to the cosmos. Many of the Giants were buried beneath mountains as punishment for their rebellion.

Virgil, a Roman poet from the 1st century B.C., in his bucolic poem *Georgics*, describes the natural world and agricultural life, often referencing mythological elements:

Virgil, *Georgics* 3.195 ff:

"When the gathered Aquilo (the North Wind) [Boreas] swoops down from the Hyperborean coasts, driving storms from Scythia and dry clouds."

NOTE: This may suggest the Romans viewed Hyperborea in a coastal area, not a landlocked one; situated just beyond Scythia.

Pliny the Elder, a Roman author from the 1st century A.D., in his comprehensive encyclopedia *Natural History*, offers a detailed description of various peoples and regions, including the mythical Hyperboreans:

Pliny the Elder, *Natural History* 4.88 ff :

"Along the Black Sea coast of Europe, as far as the river Tanais [the Don], are the Maeotae [a Scythian tribe]...and beyond them, in the rear of the Maeotae, are the Arimaspi (Arimapsians). Then come the Riphean Mountains and the region known as Peterophorus ('wing-bringers'), named so because of the feather-like snow that falls there continuously. This part of the world is cursed by nature, shrouded in dense darkness, and filled with frost and the chilly abodes of Aquilo, the North Wind known as Boreas. Beyond these mountains and Aquilo, there is said to dwell—if one can believe it—a blessed race of people called the Hyperboreans, who are famous for their longevity and legendary wonders.

It is believed that this region marks the place where the heavens pivot and the extreme cycles of the stars occur, with six months of daylight and a single day of darkness, not as some ignorant people have claimed, from the spring equinox to autumn. For these people, the sun rises once a year at midsummer and sets once at midwinter. The climate is pleasant and free from harmful winds. The natives live in the woods and groves, worship the gods both individually and collectively, and are free from discord and sorrow. Death comes to them only when they have had enough of life. After holding a banquet and anointing themselves in luxury, they leap from a specific rock into the sea, considering this form of death the most blessed.

Some authorities have placed these people not in Europe but on the nearest part of the Asian coast, as there is a similar race with similar customs, called the Attaci. Others have suggested they live between the two suns, where the sunsets of the antipodes coincide with our sunrise, but this is impossible due to the vast sea separating them. Those who describe them as living in a region with six months of daylight have noted that they sow crops in the morning, harvest at midday, gather fruit at sunset, and retreat into caves for the night. There is ample evidence of their existence, as many authorities report that they regularly sent the first fruits of their harvests to Delos as offerings to Apollo, whom they particularly worship. These offerings were initially brought by virgins, who were honored and hospitably received by the nations along the way. However, after a breach of trust, they changed the custom to leaving the offerings at the nearest border of a neighboring people, who would then pass them along until they finally reached Delos. This practice eventually ceased as well."

NOTE: Pliny's description here likely places the Hyperboreans in a region east of the Ural Mountains in an area north of the Arctic Circle. Regions fitting the description of having extreme polar day and night cycles (six months of daylight and six months of darkness) would need to be north of 66.5° North latitude, likely along the Ob, Yenisei, Lena, Kolyma, and Indigirka rivers. The **Yenisei** and **Lena** rivers are notable for their proximity to significant mountain ranges in Siberia. The Yenisei originates in the **Sayan Mountains** and flows near the **Kuznetsk Alatau** and **Eastern Sayan Mountains**, contributing to its dramatic landscapes. The Lena River flows through regions near the **Baikal Mountains** and **Verkhoyansk Range**, as well as the **Stanovoy Range**, adding to the river's rugged surroundings. The **Kolyma River** flows through the **Kolyma Mountains** in northeastern Siberia, while the **Indigirka River** passes through the **Chersky Range**. In contrast, the **Ob River** primarily traverses the flat West Siberian Plain, though its headwaters are near the **Altai Mountains**. It is also situated the closest to the site of Arkaim.

Pliny the Elder, *Natural History* 6.34:

"From the extreme north-northeast to the northernmost point where the sun rises in summer, there are the Scythians. Beyond them and outside the point where the north-northeast begins, some have placed the Hyperboreans, who are said by most authorities to be in Europe. After that point, the first known place is Lytharmis, a promontory of Celtica, and the river Carambucis, where the range of the Riphean Mountains ends and the severity of the climate lessens.

Here, we hear of a people called the Arimphaei, a race not unlike the Hyperboreans. They dwell in forests and live on berries; it is considered disgraceful for both women and men to have long hair. They are known for their gentle manners. As a result, they are reportedly considered a sacred race and are left unmolested by the fierce tribes around them. This protection also extends to those who seek refuge with them.

Beyond the Arimphaei, we find the Scythians, Cimmerians, Cissi, Anthi, Georgi, and a race of Amazons, the last of whom extend to the Caspian and Hyrcanian Seas (*Hyrcanian is for the southern shores of the Caspian Sea*)."

NOTE: This description, at first glance contradictory, would suggest a presence in Europe but also potentially east of the Caspian Sea. Beyond the Arimphaei, who are described as living in a secluded and sacred region, the geography begins to merge into more well-documented territories, blending myth with reality. The following groups are mentioned as inhabiting areas stretching from the European regions eastward towards the Caspian Sea:

- **Scythians**: These people are mentioned multiple times, indicating their widespread presence across a vast area. The Scythians were nomadic horsemen known for their fierce warrior culture, and they dominated much of the steppe regions from Eastern Europe to Central Asia.
- **Cimmerians**: An ancient people, possibly related to the Thracians, who were driven out of their homelands by the Scythians and migrated into Asia Minor. Their name became associated with the far northern regions, often in the context of dark and misty lands.

- **Cissi**: This group is less well-known, but they may represent one of the many smaller tribes living on the fringes of Scythian territory, possibly in the areas near the Caucasus or the steppes of Central Asia.
- **Anthi**: This group is not well-documented and unknown but might be related to the Antae.
- **Antae**, a people known to have lived in the region around the Black Sea, and possibly further east, in the steppe lands.
- **Georgi**: Likely a reference to the ancient people of **Georgia** (called Iberia in ancient terms), situated to the south of the Caucasus Mountains. This region was well-known for its early kingdoms and connections to both European and Asian cultures.
- **Amazons**: The Amazons, a mythical race of warrior women, were said to inhabit the lands extending towards the **Caspian** and **Hyrcanian Seas**. These tales of female warriors were often tied to the steppes and mountainous regions of Central Asia, blending myth with possible historical matriarchal societies.

Pliny's descriptions here suggest a continuum of peoples stretching from the far northern regions of Europe (possibly even into Arctic or sub-Arctic areas) through the steppes of Eastern Europe and into Central Asia, reaching as far as the Caspian and Hyrcanian Seas. The reference to the Riphean Mountains, where the climate begins to lessen in severity, might correspond to the valley regions associated with several significant mountain ranges in Eurasia. These could include the Ural Mountains, which traditionally marked the boundary between Europe and Asia, as well as the Tien Shan, Kunlun, and Altai ranges, which cradle the expansive steppes and desert basins of Central Asia. Additionally, the reference might extend to the Himalayan foothills, where the severe high-altitude climate transitions into more temperate zones. It is also noteworthy that Pliny mentions a Celtic land called Lytharmis, located beyond the Hyperboreans, along with a river that intersects a region where the Riphean mountain ranges taper off, giving way to a more temperate climate, which could provide a clue as to where ancient geographers placed Hyperborea. If we consider Pliny's description in the context of the areas around the Tarim Basin, it could represent the harsh, isolated land beyond the Hyperboreans, and would suggest either a Celtic identification in ancient times with these areas, or a misidentification with another group as Celts. The transition from the severe climates of the surrounding mountain ranges to the more temperate valleys, where rivers flow into lower elevations, might be seen as the area where the Riphean mountains end and a milder climate begins.

Seneca, a Roman philosopher and playwright from the 1st century A.D., in his tragedy *Phaedra*, describes a journey to the farthest reaches of the world:

Seneca, *Phaedra* 930 ff:

"Travel across distant, unknown nations; even if a land at the remotest edges of the world separates you, beyond the regions of Oceanus, even if you settle in the world opposite our own, even if you flee to the trembling realms of the far north and hide in its deepest corner, and even if you go beyond the reach of winter (Hyperborea) and its frosty snows, leaving behind the threatening chill of cold Boreas (the North Wind)."

Valerius Flaccus, a Roman poet from the 1st century A.D., in his epic *Argonautica*, describes the profound impact of a woman on the natural world as she travels:

Valerius Flaccus, *Argonautica* 8.209 ff (trans. Mozley):

"No lake, no river in Scythia fails to mourn her as she passes by; the very sight of her... stirred the Hyperborean snows."

Statius, a Roman poet from the 1st century A.D., in his epic *Thebaid*, uses the imagery of the Hyperborean region to evoke the harshness of the northern climates and their mythological significance:

Statius, *Thebaid* 1.694 ff (trans. Mozley):

"The frosty wagoner of the Hyperborean Bear droops languidly, with its pole slanting backward."

Ursa Major

NOTE: The "wagoner" of the **"Hyperborean Bear"** is a reference to **Ursa Major** itself, often depicted in mythology as a great bear that circles the North Star (Polaris), never setting below the horizon in northern latitudes. The **"frosty wagoner"** refers to the slow, cold, and eternal motion of the constellation around the celestial pole. In this context, **"droops languidly"** and **"with its pole slanting backward"** convey the idea of the constellation's seemingly slow and tired journey across the sky, as observed from the northern latitudes, where it appears to move in a circular motion around the North Star. This description emphasizes the eternal, almost lethargic nature of the constellation's rotation in the sky.

Statius, *Thebaid* 5.390 ff:

"Even so does Jupiter [Zeus] lash the green fields with Hyperborean snow; beasts of all kinds perish on the plains, birds are overtaken and fall dead, and the harvest is ruined by untimely frost. Then the mountains rumble, and the rivers rage."

Statius, *Thebaid* 12.650 ff:

"As when Jupiter [Zeus] strides upon the Hyperborean pole and makes the stars tremble at the approach of winter, Aeolia [the island home of the winds] is torn apart, and the storm, angry at its long inactivity, awakens. The North wind whistles with a hurricane; the mountains and waves roar, clouds clash in the dark, and thunders and crazed lightning revel."

Nonnus, a Greek poet from the 5th century A.D., in his epic *Dionysiaca*, recounts various mythological tales, including the story of Abaris:

Nonnus, *Dionysiaca* 11.132 ff (trans. Rouse):

"You have also heard of Abaris, whom Phoebus [Apollo] lifted through the air, perched on his winged, roving arrow."

Suidas, a Byzantine Greek lexicographer, compiled *The Suda* in the 10th century A.D. In it, he provides a brief description of Abaris, the legendary Hyperborean:

"Abaris: Skythian (Scythian), son of Seuthes. He wrote the so-called Skythinian Oracles and Marriage of the river Hebros and Purifications and a Theogony in prose and Arrival of Apollon among the Hyperboreans in meter. He came from Skythia (Scythia) to Greece. The legendary arrow belongs to him, the one he flew on from Greece to Hyperborean Skythia. It was given to him by Apollon. Gregory the Theologian [Christian writer C4th A.D.] mentioned this man in his Epitaphios for Basil the Great. They say that once, when there was a plague throughout the entire inhabited world, Apollon told the Greeks and barbarians who had come to consult his oracle that the Athenian people should make prayers on behalf of all of them. So, many people sent ambassadors to them, and Abaris, they say, came as ambassador of the Hyperboreans in the third Olympiad (768 BCE)."

NOTE: Although this source comes much later; it tells us that Abaris was believed to have lived in the 8th century, which seemingly contradicts other sources, where Abaris was depicted as having lived alongside Pythagoras in the 6th to 5th century BCE.

Gregory Nazianzen, a 4th-century Christian theologian, references Abaris, the legendary Hyperborean, in his writings:

"For why should I speak of the arrow of the Hyperborean Abaris, or of the Argive Pegasus, to whom flight through the air was not of such consequence...."

"You who have wings and are borne aloft, and fly like the arrows of Abaris, in order that, Cappadocian though you are, you may flee from Cappadocia."

Origen, an early Christian scholar, also mentions Abaris in his writings, questioning the purpose of his powers:

"While this was not the case either with the Proconnesian Aristeas (although Apollo would have him regarded as a god), or with the other individuals enumerated by Celsus when he says, No one regards Abaris the Hyperborean as a god, who was possessed of such power as to be borne along like an arrow from a bow. For with what object did the deity who bestowed upon this Hyperborean Abaris the power of being carried along like an arrow, confer upon him such a gift? Was it that the human race might be benefited thereby, or did he himself obtain any advantage from the possession of such a power?—always supposing it to be conceded that these statements are not wholly inventions, but that the thing actually happened through the co-operation of some demon."

Iamblichus, a Neoplatonist philosopher from the 3rd-4th century A.D., provides detailed accounts of Pythagoras's interactions with Abaris, the legendary Hyperborean, in his work *Life of Pythagoras*:

"Universally, however, it deserves to be known, that Pythagoras discovered many paths of erudition, and that he delivered an appropriate portion of wisdom conformable to the proper nature and power of each; of which the following is the greatest argument. When Abaris, the Scythian, came from the Hyperboreans, unskilled and uninitiated in the Grecian learning, and was then of an advanced age, Pythagoras did not introduce him to erudition through various theorems, but instead of silence, ausculation for so long a time, and other trials, he immediately considered him adapted to be an auditor of his dogmas, and instructed him in the shortest way in his treatise *On Nature*, and in another treatise *On the Gods*. For Abaris came from the Hyperboreans, being a priest of the Apollo who is there worshipped, an elderly man, and most wise in sacred concerns; but at that time he was returning from Greece to his own country, in order that he might consecrate to the God in his temple among the Hyperboreans, the gold which he had collected. Passing therefore through Italy, and seeing Pythagoras, he especially assimilated him to the God of whom he was the priest. And believing that he was no other than the God himself, and that no man resembled him, but that he was truly Apollo, both from the venerable indications which he saw about him, and from those which the priest had known before, he gave Pythagoras a dart which he took with him when he left the temple, as a thing that would be useful to him in the difficulties that would befall him in so long a journey. For he was carried by it, in passing through inaccessible places, such as rivers, lakes, marshes, mountains, and the like, and performed through it, as it is said, lustrations, and expelled pestilence and winds from the cities that requested him to liberate them from these evils. We are informed, therefore, that Lacedæmon, after having been purified by him, was no longer infested with pestilence, though prior to this it had frequently fallen into this evil, through the baneful nature of the place in which it was built, the mountains of Taygetus producing a suffocating heat, by being situated above the city, in the same manner as Cnossus in Crete. And many other similar particulars are related of the power of Abaris. Pythagoras, however, receiving the dart, and neither being astonished at the novelty of the thing, nor asking the reason why it was given to him, but as if he was in reality a God himself, taking Abaris aside, he showed him his golden thigh, as an indication that he was not [wholly] deceived [in the opinion he had formed of him;] and having enumerated to him the several particulars that were deposited in the temple, he gave him sufficient reason to believe that he had not badly conjectured [in assimilating him to Apollo]. Pythagoras also added, that he came [into the regions of mortality] for the purpose of remedying and benefiting the condition of mankind, and that on this account he had assumed a human form, lest men being disturbed by the novelty of his transcendency, should avoid the discipline which he possessed. He likewise exhorted Abaris to remain in that place, and to unite with him in correcting [the lives and manners] of those with whom they might meet; but to share the gold which he had collected, in common with his associates, who were led by reason to confirm by their deeds the dogma, that the possessions of friends are common. Thus, therefore, Pythagoras unfolded to Abaris, who remained with him, as we have just now said, physiology and theology in a compendious way; and instead of divination by the entrails of beasts, he delivered to him the art of prognosticating through numbers, conceiving that this was purer, more divine, and more adapted to the celestial numbers of the Gods. He delivered also to Abaris other studies which were adapted to him."

"The report, also, is very much disseminated, that he showed his golden thigh to the Hyperborean Abaris, who said that he resembled the Apollo among the Hyperboreans, and of whom Abaris was the priest; and that he did this in order that Abaris might apprehend this to be true, and that he was not deceived in his opinion. Ten thousand other more divine and more admirable particulars likewise are uniformly and unanimously related of the man: such as infallible predictions of earthquakes, rapid expulsions of pestilence and violent winds, instantaneous cessations of the effusion of hail, and a tranquillization of the waves of rivers and seas, in order that his disciples might easily pass over them. Of which things also, Empedocles the Agrigentine, Epimenides the Cretan, and Abaris the Hyperborean, receiving the power of effecting, performed certain miracles of this kind in many places. Their deeds, however, are manifest. To which we may add, that Empedocles was surnamed an expeller of winds; Epimenides, an expiator; and Abaris, a walker on air; because being carried on the dart which was given to him by the Hyperborean Apollo, he passed over rivers and seas and inaccessible places, like one walking on the air. Certain persons likewise are of opinion, that Pythagoras did the same thing, when in the same day he discoursed with his disciples at Metapontum and Tauromenium. It is also said, that he predicted there would be an earthquake from the water of a well which he had tasted; and that a ship which was sailing with a prosperous wind, would be merged in the sea. And let these, indeed, be the indications of his piety."

"But they thought that their opinions deserved to be believed, because he who first promulgated them, was not any casual person, but a God. For this was one of their questions; What was Pythagoras? For they say that he was the Hyperborean Apollo; of which this was an indication, that rising up in the Olympic games, he showed his golden thigh; and also that he received the Hyperborean Abaris as his guest; and was presented by him with the dart on which he rode through the air. But it is said that Abaris came from the Hyperborean regions, in order that he might collect gold for the temple, and that he predicted a pestilence. He also dwelt in temples, and was never seen either to eat or drink. It is likewise said, that rites which purify from evil are performed by the Lacedæmonians, and that on this account Lacedæmon was never infested with pestilence. Pythagoras, therefore, caused this Abaris to acknowledge [that he was more than man,] receiving from him at the same time the golden dart, without which it was not possible for him to find his way."

"When Abaris performed sacred rites in his accustomed manner, he procured a fore-knowledge of future events, which is studiously cultivated by all the Barbarians, through sacrificing animals, and especially birds; for they are of opinion that the viscera of such animals are subservient to a more accurate inspection. Pythagoras, therefore, not wishing to suppress his ardent pursuit of truth, but to impart it to him through a certain safer way, and without blood and slaughter, and also because he thought that a cock was sacred to the sun, furnished him with a consummate knowledge of all truth, as it is said, through the arithmetical science."

"Many instances therefore of these things might be adduced, and of upright actions frequently performed by him. But the greatest of all these, is what he said and did to Phalaris, with an invincible freedom of speech. For when he was detained in captivity by Phalaris, the most cruel of tyrants, a wise man of the Hyperborean race, whose name was Abaris, was his associate, who came to him for the sake of conversing with him, and asked him many questions, and especially such as were of a sacred nature, respecting statues and the most holy worship, the providence of the Gods, celestial and terrestrial natures, and many other things of a similar kind. But Pythagoras, being under the influence of divine inspiration, answered Abaris vehemently, and with all truth and persuasion, so as to convince those that heard him. Then, however, Phalaris was inflamed with anger against Abaris, because he praised Pythagoras, and was ferociously disposed towards Pythagoras himself. He also dared to utter blasphemies against the Gods themselves, and such as he was accustomed to pour forth. But Abaris gave Pythagoras thanks for what he said; and after this, learnt from him that all things are suspended from and governed by the heavens; which he evinced to be the case from many other things, and also from the energy of sacred rites. And Abaris was so far from thinking that Pythagoras, who taught these things, was an enchanter, that he beyond measure admired him as if he had been a God. To these things, however, Phalaris replied by endeavouring to subvert divination, and openly denying the efficacy of the things which are performed in sacred rites. But Abaris transferred the discourse from these particulars to such as are clearly apparent to all men; and endeavoured to persuade him that there is a divine providence, from those circumstances which transcend all human hope and power, whether they are immense wars, or incurable diseases, or the corruption of fruits, or the incursions of pestilence, or certain other things of the like kind, which are most difficult to be borne, and deplorable, arising from the beneficent energies of certain dæmoniacal and divine powers. Phalaris, however, shamelessly and audaciously opposed what was said. Again therefore Pythagoras, suspecting that Phalaris intended to put him to death, but at the same time knowing that he was not destined to die by Phalaris, began to address him with great freedom of speech. For looking to Abaris he said, that a transition was naturally adapted to take place from the heavens to aerial and terrestrial beings. And again, he showed that all things follow the heavens, from instances most known to all men."

Porphyry, a Neoplatonist philosopher from the 3rd century A.D., provides an account of Pythagoras's extraordinary abilities and his connection to Abaris the Hyperborean in his work *Life of Pythagoras*:

"Verified predictions of earthquakes are handed down, also that he immediately chased a pestilence, suppressed violent winds and hail, calmed storms both on rivers and on seas, for the comfort and safe passage of his friends. As their poems attest, the like was often performed by Empedocles, Epimenides, and Abaris, who had learned the art of doing these things from him. Empedocles, indeed, was surnamed Alexanemos, as the chaser of winds; Epimenides, Cathartes, the lustrator. Abaris was called Aethrobates, the walker in air; for he was carried in the air on an arrow of the Hyperborean Apollo, over rivers, seas, and inaccessible places. It is believed that this was the method employed by Pythagoras when on the same day he discoursed with his friends at Metapontum and Tauromenium."

So, having reviewed the extent of ancient sources related to Hyperborea, what can we say about the potential locations for Hyperborea?

Well, there's the site of Arkaim that was briefly mentioned in the preface. Some point to it as a candidate for the location of Hyperborea, based on ancient descriptions placing it northeast of the Scythians. Arkaim, known in Russian as Аркаим, is a fortified archaeological site dating back to approximately 2150-1650 BCE. It is associated with the Sintashta culture and is located in the steppe of the Southern Urals, specifically about 5.10 miles north-northwest of the village of Amursky and 1.43 miles east-southeast of the village of Alexandrovsky in the Chelyabinsk Oblast of Russia, just north of the Kazakhstan border. The site was discovered in 1987 by a team of archaeologists. The construction of Arkaim is attributed to the early Proto-Indo-Iranian speakers of the Sintashta culture, a group that some scholars believe represents the proto-Indo-Iranians before their eventual migration to Central Asia, and from there to regions such as Persia, India, and beyond.

In the summer of 1987, archaeologists, led by Gennady Zdanovich, were tasked with assessing the archaeological significance of a valley at the confluence of the Bolshaya Karaganka and Utyaganka rivers in southern Chelyabinsk Oblast. This was a region where construction of a reservoir had begun the previous autumn. Though some archaeological sites were already known in the area, they were considered of little importance and not considered worth preserving. However, on June 20, two students involved in the expedition, Aleksandr Voronkov and Aleksandr Ezril, reported finding unusual embankments in the steppe. This discovery was quickly recognized by Zdanovich as significant, and it would later prove to be a turning point in debates over the original homeland of the Indo-Europeans. The earlier discovery of the Sintashta culture, which yielded remains of early chariots and horses, had already suggested that the Southern Urals were a key area in the development of early technology and complex civilization. The discovery of Arkaim confirmed these assumptions.

The struggle to preserve Arkaim was intense, and the archaeologists campaigned vigorously to mobilize public opinion in favor of preserving Arkaim, initially requesting that the reservoir project be delayed until 1990. Academicians and public figures rallied to their cause, and in April 1991, the Council of Ministers officially canceled the reservoir project and declared Arkaim a "historical and geographical museum."

Arkaim was a circular stronghold, consisting of two concentric bastions made of adobe with timber frames, covered with unfired clay bricks. Inside these circles, close to the bastions, stood sixty dwellings, each equipped with hearths, cellars, wells, and metallurgical furnaces. These dwellings opened onto an inner circular street paved with wood. The street was lined with a covered drainage system that included pits for water collection. At the center of the settlement was a rectangular open space. The complex had four intricately constructed entrances, each oriented toward the cardinal points.

Scholars have suggested that the structure of Arkaim may reflect cities built "reproducing the model of the universe" as described in ancient Indo-Aryan and Iranian spiritual literature, such as the Vedas and the Avesta. The site's concentric rings of walls and radial streets may parallel the city of King Yima, described in the Rigveda. The design of Arkaim is believed by many scholars to represent "the model of the universe" associated with the ancient Indo-Iranian Priest-King Yima.

The model of the universe associated with Yima, particularly in the context of ancient Indo-Iranian spiritual literature, is primarily found in the Avesta, the sacred texts of Zoroastrianism. Yima (also known as Jamshid in Persian tradition) is a significant figure in these texts, often depicted as a king with divine favor who ruled over a golden age of prosperity. For example, in the Avesta it says, "Yima made a **vara** (enclosure, fortress), a three-folded walled city, and brought into it the seeds of all living creatures. He made that **vara** with the help of the best of men, in order to save the creatures from the storm of winter that Angra Mainyu was to bring."

Originally, Arkaim was dated to the 17th and 16th centuries BCE, but it is now considered to belong to the period of 2050-1900 BCE. More than twenty similar structures, built according to comparable patterns, have been found in the larger area spanning from the Southern Urals to northern Kazakhstan, collectively referred to as the "Land of Towns."

Covering an area of approximately 220,000 square feet, Arkaim's enclosing wall had a diameter of about 520 feet and was 13 to 16 feet thick and 18 feet high. The settlement was surrounded by a 6-foot-7-inch deep moat. The complex featured four gates, with the main gate located in the west. The dwellings ranged in size from 1,200 to 1,900 square feet and were arranged in two rings—one outer ring of thirty-nine or forty dwellings and an inner ring of twenty-seven dwellings, with the doors of the outer dwellings opening onto the circular street, and the inner dwellings facing the central square. It has been estimated that Arkaim could have housed 2,500 people. Surrounding the walls of Arkaim were arable fields, 430–460 feet by 150 feet, irrigated by an intricate system of canals and ditches.

However, critics of this theory point out that the fortified walls and the broader militaristic and nomadic Sintashta culture, to which Arkaim belongs, is a strong contrast from the idyllic, peaceful society that Hyperborea is often described as in ancient texts. Its sudden destruction around 1,900 BCE, when it was burned down and deserted, lends fuel to the fire that this was not Hyperborea. The discovery of Arkaim, however, brings up the question, just how many other sites like this are buried and waiting to be discovered?

In terms of a more peaceful existence, the Tarim Basin, the British Isles, or a valley in Tibet are worth exploring. However, these rely on our current archaeological knowledge, which is spartan to say the least, with likely 99% of possible locations still unexplored or lacking field research. The original location of Hyperborean civilization is probably buried under a mound of dirt, awaiting discovery in the places that align with the clues hinted at in ancient sources.

Researchers will need to consider other factors to uncover this lost land, such as a potential location on an island around the size of Sicily and near a river, the presence of amber deposits, swans, and evidence of unique architectural features such as beeswax. Additionally, clues such as the proximity to ancient trade routes, and the presence of unique flora and fauna that might suggest a microclimate or an isolated ecological niche could be key indicators. Some ancient sources are possibly completely incorrect, so some of the clues may lead us astray as well while others might be reliable indicators based on actual traveler accounts and stories from real Hyperboreans that made it to Ancient Greece.

In regards to the British Isles, in 2005, road workers excavating an area approximately three miles southeast of Stonehenge made a remarkable discovery: the skeleton of a 15 year old boy buried around 1,500 BCE with a stunning necklace of 90 amber beads. As noted, amber is often associated with Hyperborea. Further analysis of his remains found that he was not native to Britain, but likely came from the southern Mediterranean or a much "warmer climate" based on Strontium deposits in his teeth.

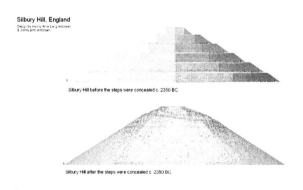

Silbury Hill, England
Design by Kenny Arne Lang Antonsen
& Jimmy john Antonsen

Silbury Hill before the steps were concealed c. 2350 BC.

Silbury Hill after the steps were concealed c. 2350 BC.

Obviously, while some might jump to conclusions of a foreigner found near Stonehenge with a necklace of amber beads, much more research would need to be done before any conclusions could be drawn. One might wish to investigate and uncover more remains near the areas around Silbury Hill, for example. Built around 2,400 BCE, it is the highest man-made prehistoric mound in Europe, and was contemporaneous with the Egyptian pyramids. At its

construction, it had a limestone exterior, much like the pyramids outer casings, and was entirely white and resembled the image to the right. Archaeologist Euan MacKie theorized that Silbury Hill was likely built by an authoritarian priesthood that controlled all of Southern Britain at the time. The image to the left is what Silbury Hill looks like today. Those at the top of the mound, and whatever rituals they may have performed, would have been seen by crowds miles around the area. Silbury Hill is estimated to have taken 18 million man hours to build, or 500 people working non-stop for 15 years. Nearby Silbury Hill lie other enigmatic monuments such as Stonehenge, Avebury, and Beckhampton

Avenue. Some researchers theorize that when viewed from above, Beckhampton Avenue may have once been designed to resemble a giant snake, similar to the famous Serpent Mound in Ohio and other serpent-like earthworks in Canada and Scotland, not to mention the crop circles that frequently appear in the fields around Avebury and Stonehenge—circles that are said to have formed

within minutes and exhibit signs of microwave radiation. The megalithic sites in Wiltshire have often been attributed to the Druids in popular imagination and films, but the truth is more complex. In reality, we know relatively little about who actually built these monuments or why, though it is likely that their construction is linked to the Early European Farmers (EEF) who arrived in Britain around 4100 BCE, similar to those who settled in other ancient sites such as Malta.

The Druids, often associated with the Celtic peoples who arrived in Britain thousands of years later during the Indo-European migrations around 2000 BCE, might have inherited some of the beliefs and practices of these earlier EEF populations. Another intriguing possibility is that the Druids were a priestly caste that existed alongside the EEF populations and persisted after the Indo-European migrations, eventually integrating with the new arrivals and continuing their spiritual traditions under the title of Druids. This theory is bolstered by similarities between Druidic beliefs and those of the Pythagoreans, especially if we consider a potential connection to the land of Hyperborea. If Hyperborea was not just a specific location but a reference to a widespread group of theocratic elites, its influence could have extended from the Tarim Basin to Siberia, the British Isles, and possibly even the Levant and Egypt. In exploring this hypothesis, Malta, with its ancient megalithic temples and possible links to early priestly traditions, might offer clues about what this ancient caste could have looked like and how their beliefs might have spread across such a vast region.

The Hypogeum in Malta is a Neolithic subterranean marvel dating back to the Saflieni phase of Maltese prehistory, between 3300 and 3000 BC. Located in Paola, this ancient structure is aptly named after the Greek word for "underground," reflecting its hidden depths beneath the earth. The Hypogeum is believed to have served both as a sanctuary and a necropolis, housing the remains of more than 7,000 individuals, as documented by archaeologists. This site stands as one of the best-preserved examples of the Maltese temple-building culture, the same civilization responsible for the creation of the Megalithic Temples and the Xagħra Stone Circle.

The Hypogeum of Ħal Saflieni was accidentally discovered in 1902 when workers constructing cisterns for a new housing development broke through its roof. Initially, the workers attempted to conceal their find, but the site's significance soon came to light. Archaeological evidence suggests that the Hypogeum may have originally been marked by a surface shrine, long since destroyed, which shielded the underground structure from discovery for millennia, which would suggest throughout the areas the Early European Farmers went, other such subterranean structures may exist, their surface entrances buried by time. The chambers, carved directly into the rock, may have begun as a natural cave, expanded over time with primitive tools. The upper chambers date back to the early phases of the Maltese Temple Period, around 4000 BC, while the lower chambers were in use until approximately 2500 BC. The

Hypogeum's design incorporates sophisticated use of light, with one chamber, known as "The Holy of Holies," aligned to be illuminated by the winter solstice. The site yielded a vast array of artifacts, including pottery, beads, and the iconic Sleeping Lady figurine, thought to symbolize a mother goddess. Among the remains of 7,000 individuals found within the Hypogeum, some skulls exhibit abnormal cranial elongation similar to those of the priestly skulls from Ancient Egypt and elsewhere. These skulls, dating back to 3000-2500 BCE, show unusual features such as missing cranial sutures, abnormally developed temporal partitions, and elongated skulls lacking a fossa median, the central seam along the top of the skull. Once displayed at the National Museum of Archaeology, the skulls were removed from public view around 1985 by Heritage Malta, the authority responsible for Malta's prehistoric heritage, and have since been available only to researchers with special permission.

Despite efforts by Heritage Malta to dismiss theories of 'serpent priests' or 'alien skulls,' the unusual characteristics of these remains have led to various interpretations. Photos and investigations by Dr. Anton Mifsud, Dr. Charles Savona Ventura, and others document the abnormality of these skulls, with some scholars drawing parallels to ancient Egyptian culture. National Geographic in the 1920s reported that Malta's earliest inhabitants were a race of long-skulled people, akin to those of early Egypt. Yet, the history of these skulls raises several unresolved questions: why were original excavation reports never published? Why were the bones of thousands of people later reduced to just a few hundred? And why were the elongated skulls removed from public view? These unanswered questions leave gaps in our understanding of Malta's ancient past, one that perhaps has connections to places as far away as the Iberian Peninsula and the British Isles as well as the construction of places such as Stonehenge.

One thing that is often drawn by researchers is that some of these elonganted skulls, like the ones in Peru that also show DNA from the Levant and Eastern Europe, have other anomalies modern science can't really explain such as possibly missing paternal DNA, and which can't be explained away through artificial cranial deformation. They were born this way.

It's worth noting that there are several genetic conditions that can result in elongated skulls. For example, a combination of Dolichocephaly with Megalencephaly could have, if selectively bred by ancient populations, resulted in a group of people with larger cranial capacities and the elongated skulls found in many ancient cultures. This group might have possessed special intellectual abilities, often observed in individuals with conditions like Autism and Megalencephaly, such as exceptional memory, heightened pattern recognition, or advanced mathematical and spatial reasoning. These traits could have been highly valued in ancient societies, potentially leading to the deliberate selection and perpetuation of these genetic characteristics to create "living computers," so to speak. Individuals with enhanced cognitive abilities, such as exceptional memory, advanced pattern recognition, and superior mathematical and spatial reasoning, could have been seen as vital assets in the governance, construction, and spiritual practices of these cultures. By selectively breeding for these traits, several ancient societies may have intentionally fostered a group of people with the intellectual capabilities necessary to perform complex tasks, manage intricate societal systems, or carry out advanced astronomical and architectural projects—functions that, in many ways, parallel the roles of modern computers, or even, when working together, as supercomputers.

If we assume, for a moment, that some of these ancient societies utilized human "supercomputers"—individuals with extraordinary cognitive abilities—hundreds of thousands of years ago, and that through sheer intellectual brainpower they developed ways to cheat death, the ancient claims of extreme longevity become less implausible. This perspective could lend a different interpretation to the Sumerian, Chinese, and other ancient accounts of people who lived for tens of thousands of years. These individuals, possessing knowledge and abilities far beyond the average human, could have been perceived as near-immortal beings—what the Ancient Greeks might have considered gods or immortals. It could also suggest they would have had the means to engineer flying devices, perhaps quite different than our own, enabling people such as Abaris the Hyperborean to travel from places such as the Tarim Basin to Delos in Ancient Greece in twelve days time.

As for the Tarim Basin, one of the notable discoveries includes the so-called "Witches of Subeshi." These mummies, found in the Subeshi area, are distinguished by their distinctive cone-shaped hats, which are tall, pointed, and made of felt. These hats are reminiscent of the stereotypical witch's hat seen in later European folklore. The rest of their attire includes long robes and intricately woven textiles, indicating a society with advanced weaving techniques resembling garments as far away as Austria at the time. The mummies were given the name "witches" due to their unusual headgear and the mysterious aura surrounding their burial practices. One of the Witches of Subeshi was found with a heavy glove on one hand, possibly

indicating she hunted with golden eagles as is seen in modern times in Kazakhstan and Kyrgyzstan. Could falconers, or those hunting using large eagles, be the source for the legend of the gold guarding griffins?

In addition, when one considers the ancient legend of Abaris, who was said to have traveled the world on

the arrow of Apollo, it raises other questions. Perhaps the modern folklore of witches riding broomsticks isn't as contemporary as we often think, nor merely related to the use of wood glazed with psychedelic substances inserted into female genitalia which made them believe they were flying, as some theories suggest. What if those practicing pagan rituals actually had access to certain types of wood that had been infected with specific insects, and which allowed for quantum effects to emerge, enabling anti-gravity and flight? This idea might sound far-fetched, but in the next section, we will explore the claims of a celebrated entomologist Viktor Grebennikov, whose work—if proven true—could suggest that ancient cultures in Siberia developed techniques that allowed for human flight. Such capabilities might explain the existence of the Paracas skulls, as it could imply that there

were people from a lost age of man who traveled the world and developed science and technology far beyond our current understanding. These people may have evolved both intellectually and genetically to a level that we would view today as alien to us, utilizing time-dilating technology that cloaks them not only from our vision but also from many of our standard evidence collection techniques. This advanced technology would allow them to remain hidden, eluding even the most intelligent of investigators and leaving only traces that appear as myths or anomalies. Such a civilization, if it existed, could operate beyond the constraints of time as we understand it, making their existence almost impossible to detect without an understanding of time dilation.

Other intriguing subjects for potential explorers to investigate include the descriptions of griffins and the one-eyed Arimaspians. Some scholars have suggested that the one-eyed Arimaspians may have been inspired by people wearing masks. Others suggest a link to the Uralic Mari people.

The origin of the griffin myth, as suggested by Adrienne Mayor

Protoceratops skull   Psittacosaurus skull

There is also a theory that the legendary griffins guarding gold may have been inspired by the fossilized remains of Protoceratops. The griffins were depicted as having the torso of a lion, and the wings and head of an eagle. Several mountain ranges from the Ural Mountains through Siberia to Tibet have been known for their rich gold deposits since ancient times, including the Urals, Altai, Sayan, and Tian Shan ranges, as well as the Kunlun and Himalayan regions. These areas have a very long history of gold mining, and their mineral wealth, combined with the discovery of fossilized remains like those of Protoceratops, may have inspired ancient legends of griffins guarding gold, especially around the Dzungarian Gate, historically known for very strong winds and as a pass between the Eurasian steppe and lands further east. This area is also rich in gold deposits and dinosaur fossils, particularly Protoceratops. Some scholars have speculated that this region might correspond to the mythical home of Boreas, the North Wind, as described by Herodotus, who related a story of gold-guarding griffins and the Hyperboreans living beyond them.

Herodotus, citing the explorer Aristeas, described the Issedones as living east of Scythia, with the one-eyed Arimaspians, gold guarding griffins, and Hyperboreans living further beyond. Some place the Issedones in Western Siberia or Xinjiang, scholars like J. D. P. Bolton and Carl Ruck suggest that Hyperborea might have been located in Siberia, beyond the Dzungarian Gate in northern Xinjiang. This might suggest a location closer to the Gobi Desert, or a similar site with fossils and gold deposits. Those that believe the Dzungarian Gate is a more probable location than the Tarim Basin often argue for it because of how dry and arid the Basin is today. However, they fail to note that conditions in the Basin 2,500 to 4,000 years ago were quite different than they are now. More importantly, that also applies to the Tarim Mummies; which may suggest the aridity is not responsible for their preservation but something else such as a substance applied to their bodies which has been overlooked by researchers.

Tadeusz Sulimirski believes that the Arimaspi were a Sarmatian tribe originating from the upper valley of the River Irtysh. Meanwhile, Dmitry Machinsky draws a different connection, linking the Arimaspi with three-eyed *ajna* figurines discovered in

the Minusinsk Depression—artifacts traditionally attributed to the Afanasevo and Okunevo cultures of southern Siberia.

Ovid's descriptions could also hint at a shamanic ritual in which participants attached feathers to their bodies, possibly symbolizing a connection with birds. The gold-guarding griffins, rather than being literal creatures, might have been a tribe of people adorned in elaborate costumes or masks, possibly intended to intimidate or signify their role as protectors of valuable resources.

However, alternative explanations exist, such as the possibility that these stories were inspired by real animals, like a species of eagle or another large bird with a significant wingspan. Over the last 100 years, there have been numerous reported sightings of giant birds across the globe, often described as having massive wingspans far exceeding those of known species. In the United States, the "Thunderbird" is a recurring figure in these reports. In 1977, in Lawndale, Illinois, three boys claimed they were attacked by two giant birds, one of which allegedly picked up a ten-year-old boy and carried him for a short distance before dropping him. This incident, coupled with an earlier sighting in 1948 in Alton, Illinois, where witnesses described a bird with a 25-foot wingspan, has fueled local legends. Similar sightings occurred in South Texas in 1976, where residents reported encounters with a creature dubbed "Big Bird," described as having a wingspan of 12 to 15 feet and leathery, bat-like skin.

Outside the U.S., giant bird sightings have also been reported in remote parts of the world. In Papua New Guinea, locals and explorers have described encounters with the "Ropen," a creature resembling a giant bird or pterosaur with a wingspan of up to 20 feet, with reports dating back to the 1930s. Similarly, in Zambia, the "Kongamato" is a creature said to inhabit swamps and is often described as a large, reddish bird or bat with a wingspan of 4 to 7 feet, though some reports suggest much larger sizes. In Alaska, numerous reports throughout the late 20th century describe "Thunderbirds" with wingspans of 14 to 18 feet, often seen flying over remote areas or coastlines. Additionally, the infamous "Mothman" sightings in West Virginia between 1966 and 1967, though often described as more humanoid, involved a creature with large wings and an estimated wingspan of 10 to 12 feet, and has been seen more recently in the Midwest in the Chicagoland and Rockford, Illinois areas.

The story below from a bird forum describes a sighting in western Wisconsin in 2009 that suggests that there may be bird species in the wild, likely endangered and still unknown to science, that could be the original source for the legend of the Griffins:

> "A few years ago my girlfriend and I were canoeing in the Willow River State Park in Western Wisconsin. From across the lake we noticed something large in a tree. We couldn't quite make it out but my first thought was that it was a bird because I could see the tips of the wings hanging down. We began paddling towards it and as we got closer we began to question whether or not it could possibly be a bird. It simply looked too large to be a bird. I thought it was a big nest that had begun to fall apart or something like that hanging in the tree. Then we got close enough to spook it and it raised it's head which had been tucked away and spread it's wings. I was absolutely shocked at the size of it. It was all one color, dark brown, and it looked like it could have been a Golden Eagle. Now I realize that perception can be misleading and it's difficult to judge size from a distance, but I made a visual mark on the tree from it's feet to the tip of it's head and then went right up next to the tree after it had flown away. I did the same thing for the wingspan as it spread it's wings next to some protruding branches. My best guess is that this bird stood 5 feet tall and had a wingspan of over 10 feet. I do realize how ridiculous that sounds. Go ahead and call me crazy, or just assume that I'm over estimating the size, but I know what I saw. When it flew away the wings flapped like nothing I have ever seen or heard. They flapped unbelievably slow an powerfully and made a very loud swooshing noise. Each flap of it's wings took 5 seconds to complete and it sounded like someone was blowing as hard as they could right in my ear. It was truly a wonder to behold and anyone else who had been there would have said the same thing. I have seen many large Golden Eagles before and they didn't even come close to comparing to this. It looked to be almost twice the size of the largest Golden Eagle possible. I do not believe that an Eagle could ever get that large and I don't believe it was an Eagle. I had considered a Condor, but a Condor in WI? No way! The head was clearly brown as well, and even Condors don't

get that big. The beak was hard to make out, but I think it was straighter and darker than a typical Eagle. Also, the Golden Eagles that I have seen had patches of golden or amber colors. This bird was a very dark brown throughout with no patchiness. It even looked black from a distance. Anyway, I'm just wondering if anyone else has ever seen anything like this? What could it have been? Can an Eagle get that big? What is your best explanation for what we saw? If there is anyone out there investigating extraordinarily large bird sightings, my girlfriend and I would like to give an official statement."

THE BIGGEST KNOWN FLYING BIRD - ARGENTAVIS MAGNIFICENS

Other stories exist, for example, this one from the Fortean Times:

"Apart from sighting reports of the Thunderbird of Native American lore, the Jersey Devil, Mothman – and conventional-looking giant birds, such as those seen in Alaska in 2002 [FT166:6] – some modern reports of giant winged creatures in the US do sound like pterosaurs; and there are reports of flying sharp-toothed lizards with bat-like wings from many parts of Africa.

Following the 1975 discovery of a fossilized pterosaur skeleton with a wingspan of 51ft (15.5m) in Big Bend National Park, Texas, there was a run of sighting reports across Texas – although "big bird" sightings had been occurring in the state for at least 30 years. Witnesses in the early months of 1976 described enormous winged creatures with bat-like wings and a face like a cat's. For example: on 24 February, three elementary school teachers, driving to work in San Antonio, saw a huge "bird" with a wingspan of 15–20ft (4.6–6m) or more swoop over their cars, no higher than a telephone line. "I could see the skeleton of this bird through the skin or feathers or whatever," said Patricia Bryant, "and it stood out black against the background of the grey feathers." David Rendon added that the creature glided rather than flew and that the huge wings had a bony structure. Later they found the "bird" illustrated in an encyclopædia, where it was captioned "pteranodon".

Ken Gerhard, a cryptozoologist from San Antonio, Texas, who has written a book on giant winged creatures, suggests that some of them could be Argentinian pteratorns, (Argentavis magnificens), giant birds of prey with wingspans of over 25ft (7.6m), which survived much more recently than pterosaurs. "These are the surviving ancestors of modern condors and vultures," he said. "They lived up to 6,000 years ago, we know for sure, in parts of North America. In fact, over 100 specimens have been recovered from the La Brea tar pits in California." San Antonio (TX) Express, 28 July 2007. "

If such giant birds exist, the question then arises: why haven't we found them? One possible explanation is that these birds may inhabit extremely remote and inaccessible regions, such as dense rainforests, vast mountain ranges, or uncharted wilderness areas in Siberia, Alaska or Canada where human presence is minimal. In these isolated environments, large creatures could easily avoid detection, especially if their populations are small and scattered. Additionally, if these birds are primarily nocturnal or have evolved to be highly elusive, their chances of being observed by humans would be even lower. Their potential rarity, combined with behavior that allows them to detect and avoid humans from a distance, could explain why sightings are so rare and why they remain undiscovered by modern science.

Another factor could be the small population sizes of these hypothetical birds. If their numbers are critically low, they might be spread across large, remote areas, further reducing the likelihood of human encounters. Reports of giant birds might also be frequently dismissed as misidentifications of known species, optical illusions, or exaggerations, leading to blind dismissals and skepticism within the scientific community. Without physical evidence, such as feathers, bones, or other biological samples, which often degrade quickly in the wild, these reports are often not taken seriously. Moreover, the lack of resources for conducting rigorous scientific expeditions in these remote regions limits the chances of discovering such species. Until actual evidence is found, the existence of these birds remains a mystery, occupying a surreal space between myth and potential reality.

Much like other cryptids such as the Loch Ness Monster and Bigfoot, it is possible that these giant birds are not merely elusive animals but represent an advanced form of intelligent life that has developed the ability to cloak itself from human detection. Those that support this theory question if these beings intentionally avoid human contact by manipulating spacetime—specifically through time dilation. By altering their temporal experience, they could exist in a state where they are effectively invisible to us, entering our everyday reality only for brief periods and for purposes that remain largely unknown to us.

These temporal excursions could be driven by a variety of motivations, such as curiosity, nostalgia, the need to exchange atmosphere, or the collection of specific resources from our environment that are inaccessible when they are in a time-dilated state. This ability to step in and out of our temporal experience would explain the sporadic and fleeting nature of sightings, as well as the lack of physical evidence. They could also represent evidence of genetic engineering in the Earth's past, and where the ability to enter into a time dilated environment is built into their genetic code. And while all of this may seem like wild speculation not based on any physical evidence; the truth is: *it really is not*. There is video and photographic evidence of cryptid and other sightings such as UFOs, which likely imply time dilating technology, a wealth of reliable eyewitness testimony, and significant evidence that military or government authorities have systematically engaged in efforts to suppress the truth and discredit those who speak out. Numerous whistleblowers have come forward with accounts of disinformation campaigns orchestrated by powerful institutions, which have used media outlets and legal systems as tools to ridicule and silence those who challenge the official narratives. For instance, Bob Lazar, who in 1989 publicly claimed to have worked on reverse-engineering extraterrestrial technology at a site near Area 51, has faced decades of ridicule and discreditation efforts. Lazar reported being harassed and threatened, with his academic and employment records mysteriously vanishing, making it difficult for him to prove his credentials and work history.

Similarly, Philip Corso, a former U.S. Army officer, authored *The Day After Roswell*, in which he claimed to have been involved in the government's cover-up of alien technology recovered from the Roswell crash. After his book's publication, Corso faced intense scrutiny and attempts to discredit his military service and personal credibility. Despite his distinguished career, including his work in the Eisenhower administration, Corso's revelations were largely dismissed by mainstream media, and he was often portrayed as a fringe conspiracy theorist.

In another case, Gary McKinnon, a British hacker who in 2002 accessed U.S. military and NASA computers searching for evidence of UFOs, claimed to have found files related to extraterrestrial technology and off-world military personnel, specifically he claimed:

"I knew that governments suppressed antigravity, UFO-related technologies, free energy or what they call zero-point energy. This should not be kept hidden from the public when pensioners can't pay their fuel bills...A NASA photographic expert said that there was a Building 8 at Johnson Space Center where they regularly airbrushed out images of UFOs from the high-resolution satellite imaging. I logged on to NASA and was able to access this department. They had huge, high-resolution images stored in their picture files. They had filtered and unfiltered, or processed and unprocessed, files.

My dialup 56K connection was very slow trying to download one of these picture files. As this was happening, I had remote control of their desktop, and by adjusting it to 4-bit color and low screen resolution, I was able to briefly see one of these pictures. It was a silvery, cigar-shaped object with geodesic spheres on either side. There were no visible seams or riveting. There was no reference to the size of the object and the picture was taken presumably by a satellite looking down on it. The object didn't look manmade or anything like what we have created. Because I was using a Java application, I could only get a screenshot of the picture -- it did not go into my temporary internet files. At my crowning moment, someone at NASA discovered what I was doing and I was disconnected."

McKinnon's actions led to a high-profile legal battle, with the U.S. government seeking his extradition and prosecution under anti-terrorism laws. Despite his claims that his motives were purely to uncover the truth, McKinnon faced severe legal threats, including extradition and life imprisonment, highlighting the lengths to which these authorities will go to suppress this information.

Crop circle researchers have reported similar experiences of suppression and disinformation. They claim that two men, Doug Bower and Dave Chorley, were hired or encouraged to create fake crop circles in order to divert attention away from genuine formations, the latter which often appeared under mysterious conditions. These authentic crop circles reportedly formed within seconds or minutes and featured complex, advanced designs, many of which were linked to Pythagorean symbols. Additionally, these formations exhibited physical signs, such as altered plant structures and the presence of microwave radiation, suggesting that their creation was due to advanced technology rather than people with boards. However, in addition to the two men, mainstream media was also utilized to only show the fake ones in order to ridicule anyone that suggested there might be real ones not being created by bored pranksters.

One particularly intriguing example is the Chilbolton Crop Circle, which appeared next to the Chilbolton Radio Telescope in Hampshire, England, in August 2001. This crop circle is especially noteworthy because it seemed to be a response to the Arecibo message sent into space in 1974. The Arecibo message was a binary-coded message containing basic information about humanity and Earth, intended for any potential extraterrestrial civilizations that might receive it. The Chilbolton Crop Circle mimicked this format but included significant alterations. The message in the crop circle depicted a figure with a larger head and smaller body, interpreted as an alien being, and described a civilization that purportedly exists on Earth, Mars, and four moons of Jupiter, mirroring a description handed down to us by the Sumerians, who believed the Annukaki came from a moon of Jupiter (and not as a mysterious planet X as is often claimed as that is due to a misunderstanding that fails to take into account that the Sumerians counted moons as planets). Additionally, the message suggested that these beings possess a

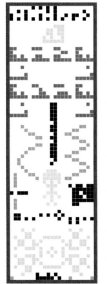

triple helix DNA structure, in contrast to the double helix DNA of humans.

These findings were dismissed by mainstream media and labeled as hoaxes, despite the fact that actual researchers believe the complexity and precision of these crop circles exceeds what could be achieved by any two individuals alone within a time frame that some claim would have been within several minutes. Other researchers have sought to explain them away as non-intelligent weather phenomona. The dismissal of such phenomena, paired with the intentional creation of fake crop circles, points to a deliberate attempt to prevent serious investigation into what might be evidence of an advanced intelligence.

The reason this is mentioned isn't so much because this could be a possible explanation for descriptions of gold-guarding Griffins, but because genetic engineering could be evidence for the existence of advanced technology and civilization in our remote past—and potential evidence of a lost age of man. One of the most intriguing pieces of evidence that some point to as support for this theory is the Paracas skulls that were mentioned earlier. These elongated skulls, discovered in the Paracas region of Peru, are claimed by some people to be physical evidence of the biblical Nephilim.

The Nephilim are described in the Book of Genesis as the offspring of the "sons of God" and the "daughters of men." They are often depicted as giants or beings of great stature and power. This has led some researchers to propose that the Paracas skulls, with their unusual shape and size, might be these ancient beings that became known as the Nephilim.

The Paracas skulls are distinct for their extreme elongation, which some have argued cannot be fully explained by the traditional practice of head binding, a cultural practice known to have been performed by various ancient civilizations to alter the shape of the skull. Proponents of the Nephilim theory suggest that the volume and cranial capacity of some of these skulls exceed what would be possible through cranial deformation alone, implying that they might belong to a different species or a hybrid race. However, the problem with this theory is, that in order to mate with a human, you need to be human, or at least close enough to one like a Neanderthal in order to create a hybrid. This could imply these "sons of God" that "bred with the daughters of man" were not metaphysical beings removed from physical reality but a distinct branch of the homo sapiens family that had evolved beyond us, either through natural selection over hundreds of thousands of years, or through artificial selection across tens of thousands of years, much as dogs were bred selectively from wolves, but were still close enough to us genetically to breed. There are other much more terrifying conclusions one could draw as well, but without more evidence, the truth is: any hypotheses we draw up remain in the domain of pure speculation, and no one can say with certainty that these elongated skulls are evidence for genetic engineering, or are in any way linked to Hyperborea or an advanced civilization in the past, but they do represent a curious anomaly, and one that begs many questions.

Skeptics will say at this point, "Well, these anomalies are likely errors, and this is all just wild speculation, pseudo-science, and pure insanity." But is it? Let's take the case of the Atacama Skeleton.

This skeleton was found in the Atacama Desert in Chile. It exhibits more mutations than any currently known, and for years, it was believed to be the remains of an extraterrestrial being until DNA testing revealed it was, in fact, human. Much like the Paracas and Malta skulls, it exhibits elongation of the skull and other genetic traits not generally found in modern human populations such as an unusual number of ribs. When you take cases such as this into account, along with the other enigmatic skulls—like those found in the Aleutians and other locations—that have 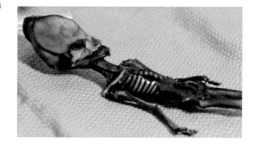 been removed from the public view and made inaccessible to researchers, and consider the findings that are often ridiculed or ignored by mainstream media and scientists, it raises important questions. These are questions that deserve to be asked and thoroughly investigated via serious scientific inquiry.

Another legend associated with Hyperborea is that of Perseus. According to Pindar, Perseus is said to have journeyed to Hyperborea on his way to slay Medusa. Perseus, much like Abaris, was also believed to be able to fly as well as receiving a helmet of invisibility. The Gorgons were often depicted as living in the far west, at the edge of the world, in a place that was remote and difficult to reach. Some sources place them near the land of the Hesperides, another mythical location in the far west where the golden apples of immortality grew. It is believed that the Gorgon myth is related to the Sumerian myth of Humbaba, the guardian of the Cedar Forest, who had the power to "stun" Gilgamesh. In the Epic of Gilgamesh, Humbaba's terrifying gaze was said to paralyze his enemies, and those who encountered him often experienced missing time or found themselves in a different location after the encounter. This ability to incapacitate is reminiscent of the later Greek myth of Medusa, who could turn people to stone merely by making eye contact with them.

One location where similar phenomena has been seen today is a place known as Skinwalker Ranch in Utah. Researchers there have uncovered evidence of things such as possible dire wolves, believed to have been extinct since 8,000 BCE. Researchers have also discovered potential evidence of time dilating phenomena, including orbs that appear for only a single frame, resembling the geodesic spheres Gary McKinnon claimed to have seen in NASA files. These orbs have also been reported in the sky in connection with cattle deaths and mutilations, accompanied by strange gamma ray radiation and other magnetic, electronic and GPS anomalies. Additionally, signs of an underground device have been discovered, shaped like a donut and closely resembling the hypothetical blueprint for physicist Amos Ori's time machine. According to Ori's design, one could only travel back to the point when the device was first activated. This implies that if a time machine exists beneath the sands of Utah, it was likely constructed around 10,000 BCE or earlier. Such a discovery could point to evidence of a lost age of humanity, an era that advanced scientifically far beyond our own before being obliterated by a catastrophic event, echoing the ancient myths and legends of a great flood that wiped out nearly all life except for a few survivors who were forewarned. What could provide such a warning? Well, the ability to travel forward and then back through time would allow one to have knowledge of the future, including events that would destroy one's civilization, allowing one to plan ahead so something might survive. This might include building sites such as Stonehenge, which some claim, within its layout, show a knowledge of the atomic ratio of hydrogen, and contain Ancient Egyptian hieroglyphics, which when translated, state, "Eternally living Atum". Interestingly, some claim that at the end of World War II, the Nazis funneled all their remaining resources into a highly secretive project believed to be critical to their war effort. This project, allegedly known as Die Glocke or "The Bell," is thought by some to have been a time machine. According to these theories, the design for this device was inspired by ancient technologies or knowledge that the Nazis had recovered from Tibet, India, or Sanskrit sources, and was connected to a circular industrial structure resembling Stonehenge. These claims suggest that the Nazis were attempting to harness advanced antediluvian technology, believing it could turn the tide of the war in their favor but were unable to finish the project due to unexpected side effects, such as the flesh melting off people's faces that were by it, and many others dying. In his 2001 book *The Hunt for Zero Point*, Nick Cook traced the origins of the Die Glocke ("The Bell") legend to

Igor Witkowski's 2000 book *Prawda o Wunderwaffe* ("The Truth About The Wonder Weapon"). Witkowski described Die Glocke as a bell-shaped device, roughly 4 meters high and 3 meters in diameter, developed by Nazi scientists. The device allegedly featured two high-speed, counter-rotating cylinders filled with a purplish, metallic liquid known as "Xerum 525." According to these accounts, Die Glocke had antigravitational effects and was rumored to be a time machine or part of an SS antigravity program for a weapon of mass destruction that could win the war. Cook further suggested that SS official Hans Kammler traded this technology to the U.S. military in exchange for his freedom at the end of the war.

Witkowski claimed to have found evidence of Die Glocke through declassified WWII-era documents from the Polish government, including an affidavit from the war crimes trial of General Jakob Sporrenberg, who supposedly confessed to ordering the murder of those involved in the project. The Bell was allegedly developed under a division of the Waffen-SS in Lower Silesia, with experimentation accelerating toward the end of the war as it was deemed more critical than any other project for winning the war. Prisoners from the Gross-Rosen concentration camp were reportedly exposed to radiation from the device, leading to numerous deaths and symptoms such as severe burns, hair loss, bleeding, and acute radiation sickness. Witkowski speculated that Xerum 525 was an irradiated form of mercury, potentially used to create a plasma capable of distorting spacetime. Some have even speculated that this material could be the infamous *Red Mercury*, a purported Soviet-era invention. Allegedly, it was a unique blend of Mercury, Plutonium, Antimony, and other elements, believed to enable the creation of fusion-sized bombs compact enough to fit in a small ball. While some argue that *Red Mercury* was merely a decoy in a covert operation to trap terrorists attempting to build atomic weapons, others, including Samuel T. Cohen, the developer of the neutron bomb, believed Red Mercury was real. Cohen asserted that the Soviets had successfully constructed many fusion bombs using this strangely superconductive substance.

In the context of the Early European Farmers (EEF) populations, who are thought to have built Stonehenge and other megalithic sites, it is interesting that around 5,000 years ago, ancient Iberians were believed to have ingested cinnabar, a red mercury sulfide mineral shown to the right. Cinnabar is basically a rock that has mercury in it, and we know they ingested or inhaled it because these people have been found with extremely toxic levels. Despite its known toxicity, cinnabar was highly valued in ancient times and in some places such as Iberia, used in burial rituals, where it slows decomposition. It was ground into a powder and either ingested or applied to the dead as part of ceremonial practices. Interestingly, cinnabar remains in use today in regions like Tibet, the Caribbean and South Africa, where it is believed to have "magical effects" and also in China, where it is included in over 40 alternative healing recipes to treat brain injuries and other ailments. The latter binds it molecularly with other agents that in small doses may actually treat various conditions on a cellular level but in larger doses, becomes toxic, and likely even fatal. So, the question is, why would people in Iberia, the same Early European Farmers responsible for building Stonehenge, have ingested a substance that likely would have resulted in serious physical and unpleasant reactions such as hair loss, kidney failure, tremors, memory loss and more? The reasonable explanation is that, much like in Tibet or China, they found a use for it, one that led to their bodies having 1,000 as much mercury as one might expect. Perhaps another explanation might be responsible for the high levels of mercury in these people, and that it relates to a ritual that was similar to the experiment the Nazis might have been performing in Lower Silesia in 1944, reported to have used a form of mercury to manipulate spacetime.

Why would anyone want to manipulate spacetime, especially in 3000 BCE? For the priests of that era, it might have been a way to touch the divine and bring their spirituality to life by demonstrating the reality of their beliefs. In our time, these beliefs seem like pure fiction because the reality of something described is much more questionable than a reality one has experienced. Many of us, myself included, have become atheists because religious stories often appear to be the inventions of people who lacked scientific understanding, creating explanations for things they did not comprehend. *But what if we're wrong?* What if some of these stories had a basis in reality at one point, though changed and corrupted over thousands of years, and still represent something real today: *once understood through the proper scientific and technological lens?*

Consider the religion of the Ancient Egyptians, who believed that at death, one traveled to another world and had to pass a series of tests based on how one lived. Success meant entering a new life, while failure meant one's brain would be devoured. Imagine if a technologically advanced civilization in our past, likely human, sought to conquer death by manipulating spacetime and entering a dimension of altered time. They might transfer their consciousness into genetically engineered bodies that do not require food or water, do not age, and are adapted to thrive in a time-dilated environment—perhaps with wings for flight. In such an environment, larger eyes with hardened corneas, possibly black or red, would be necessary to see in infrared, as visible light would shift into infrared through a bubble of time dilation.

Living in such a world, they might watch over human civilization, seeing us as we see photos, stuck in time, or if they watched long enough, as slowly moving like in a slow motion video, with every second of our time passing as hours in theirs. Perhaps this world is where they grant new life at death, offering an entrance to this underworld to those who have earned it. This world could be an "ark," preserving all life worth preserving as information within technology that appears to us as something such as a crystal skull, where one perceives oneself to exist in a new life, but in reality, exists solely as information in a crystalline structure consisting of quartz. Quartz, a form of silicon dioxide, could theoretically serve as a medium for storing vast amounts of information. Quartz crystals have the capacity to encode and store

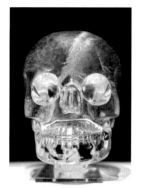

data through a process known as 3D holographic storage, where information is inscribed in the crystal's internal structure using light, such as laser technology. The data would be stored in the form of patterns or interference patterns within the crystal lattice, potentially allowing for enormous amounts of information to be preserved in a stable, long-lasting medium.

Moreover, the atomic structure of quartz could be manipulated at the quantum level, utilizing the principles of quantum computing and quantum entanglement to store and process information far beyond the capabilities of conventional digital systems. In such a system, an entire consciousness, along with memories, experiences, and even the essence of life, could theoretically be encoded as complex quantum states within the crystal. Both scenarios, while speculative, would allow a civilization to preserve not just life in its physical form but the informational blueprint of a life itself, offering a digital or virtual existence that could be perceived as reality by the consciousness encoded within the quartz.

If a civilization in the past became sufficiently advanced, it's conceivable that they could have, with enough determination, created a "heaven" beyond the constraints of our normal experience of time, and even a "hell" they banished others to. These realms, though imperceptible to us, might be interwoven with our reality through a manipulation of gravity and time. As Shakespeare famously said, "There are more things in heaven and earth than are dreamt of in your philosophy." When one takes those words and applies it to our current scientific paradigms, it suggests our understanding of the universe is just getting started, and that there may be altered dimensions of space and time that we have yet to grasp—realms that advanced humans from a lost age of man opened, explored and conquered in ways we

cannot yet fathom, and which are only known to us through the myths and legends of our earliest remembered cultures. Myths that could be related to the modern reports of UFOs, cryptids and the paranormal, such as this orb of light that was reported to have descended above the Temple Mount on January 28th, 2011 in Jerusalem and hovered above where the Ark of the Covenant was believed to have been seated before shooting up into the sky in the blink of an eye. Although it is always possible this video itself could have been a hoax, there are hundreds of thousands of other videos, photos and witness reports of similar phenomena that are not.

Part 2: On Viktor Grebennikov's Flying Machine

"The day science begins to study non-physical phenomena, it will make more progress in one decade than in all the previous centuries of its existence. To understand the true nature of the universe, one must think it terms of energy, frequency, and vibration."

Nikola Tesla

As mentioned in the previous chapter, one of the ways the descriptions of Abaris the Hyperborean flying across the known world on an arrow could be explained is through the claims of Viktor Grebennikov. In the summer of 1988, Viktor Stepanovich Grebennikov, an entomologist based in Novosibirsk, wrote that he made a startling discovery while examining the microstructure of a beetle's wing case under a microscope. He was confused by an "unusually rhythmic, highly ordered, multidimensional honeycomb-like pattern." While handling a chitin bristle from this beetle's shell, he noticed that it mysteriously hovered in the air after slipping out of his tweezers. He conducted further experiments, tying several chitin plates together with wire and arranging them vertically. To his surprise, even the lightest object, like a thumbtack, would be repelled and pushed aside when placed on the block. When he managed to fix the thumbtack on top of the chitin block, it lifted off and briefly became invisible and vanished from sight.

Over the next three years, Grebennikov dedicated himself to studying this bio-antigravity effect, developing the design for a new kind of platform and conducting numerous experiments. With the help of Professor V. Zolotarev, he filed a patent application for his invention. By 1991, Grebennikov had successfully built his Gravity Plane, a noiseless and inertialess aircraft capable of reaching speeds between 930 and 1,500 miles per hour. The aircraft was nearly invisible from the ground, with observers seeing only a light sphere, disc, or sharply outlined cloud where the plane was.

Despite the significance of his discovery, Grebennikov found it challenging to gain recognition from the scientific community, which largely ignored his work. He passed away in April 2001 after suffering a stroke, leaving behind his 1997 book "My World," where he detailed his findings and experiences.

Rather than summarize the rest of his story, it's best to allow Grebennikov to tell his story in his own words. Below, I have provided a translated section from his book *My World*, specifically Chapter V, where he describes how he discovered and built a flying machine from the chitin of an endangered insect species in Siberia. It is important to note that these claims should be considered unsubstantiated until they have been scientifically and experimentally verified. This verification might be difficult, as Grebennikov intentionally chose not to disclose the specific insect species that was central to his discovery, out of concern that it could face extinction if widely known. Additionally, it has been suggested that Soviet authorities heavily censored his work, removing 200 pages of content and permitting him to publish only what was already publicly available in the newspapers and magazines of the time. There are also reports that Grebennikov demonstrated his flying machine at the Siberian Research Institute of Agriculture and Agricultural Chemistry. However, identifying this insect, procuring a species, and rigorously testing and documenting his design would be the most important step to confirm the validity of his claims.

Chapter V: "Flight" by Viktor Grebennikov

Part One

It was a quiet evening on the steppe, with the copper-red sun just grazing the distant, misty horizon. I had lingered too long with my insect-related work and it was too late to return home. I prepared to spend the night under the open sky. Fortunately, I still had water in my flask and some mosquito repellent—essential here by the steep bank of the salty lake, where the air buzzed with countless mosquitoes. This was the Kamyshlov Valley, once a powerful tributary of the Irtysh River, now reduced to a deep, wide gully dotted with salty lakes, a consequence of plowing the steppes and cutting down the forests.

The air was perfectly still—not a blade of grass stirred. Above the evening lake, flocks of ducks flitted about, and the distant whistles of sandpipers could be heard. The high, pearl-colored sky arched over the serene steppe. It felt good to be here, surrounded by the vast, open spaces.

I settled down at the edge of the cliff, on a grassy patch: I spread out my cloak and used my backpack as a pillow. Before lying down, I gathered a few dry cow patties, stacked them nearby, and lit them, releasing a warm, familiar scent that drifted lazily over the sleepy steppe. Stretching out on my simple bed, I relished the comfort of the open air and anticipated another rare, wonderful night on the steppe.

The blue smoke gently lulled me toward sleep, carrying me off to the Land of Fairy Tales. Sleep came quickly—I felt as small as an ant, then as vast as the sky. But tonight, these shifts in my body's perceived size were unusually intense, coupled with a new sensation: a sudden, terrifying feeling of falling, as if the high bank beneath me had vanished, leaving me to plunge into an unknown abyss.

Then came the flickering lights. I opened my eyes, expecting them to vanish, but they persisted, dancing across the pearl-silver sky, the lake, and the grass. A sharp metallic taste filled my mouth, like I had touched my tongue to a powerful battery. My ears buzzed, and I could hear the double beats of my heart, pounding clearly. Sleep was impossible now.

I sat up, trying to shake off the strange sensations, but they clung to me. The flickers in my eyes morphed from wide, blurry flashes to narrow, sharp lines—like sparks or chains—distorting my view of the world around me.

Then I remembered: I had felt something similar years ago in a small grove, the Enchanted Grove.

I had to move. I got up and walked along the shore to see if the effect persisted. Right near the cliff, there was a definite influence of "something." But as I moved a few meters deeper into the steppe, that "something" noticeably faded.

I began to feel a bit uneasy, alone in the deserted steppe by the "Enchanted Lake." The thought of quickly packing up and leaving crossed my mind, but curiosity won out. What was happening here? Could it be the smell of the lake water and algae? I decided to investigate and went down to the bottom of the cliff, sitting by the water on a large lump of clay. The thick, sweetish smell of sapropel—the decaying remains of algae—wrapped around me like a mud bath. I stayed there for five minutes, then ten—nothing unpleasant happened. It seemed like I could sleep here, but the dampness made it unappealing.

I climbed back up the cliff, and the strange sensations returned. My head spun, the "galvanic" taste reappeared in my mouth, and my sense of weight fluctuated—I felt incredibly light at times, and unbearably heavy at others. The flickers danced in my eyes again.

It didn't add up: if this were truly a "cursed place" or some kind of anomaly, the thick grass wouldn't be growing here, and those large bees wouldn't be nesting in such great numbers. The steep, clayey cliff was riddled with their burrows, and I had unknowingly settled down to sleep right above their underground "bee city," with its countless tunnels, chambers, larvae, and pupae—all thriving.

At the time, I couldn't make sense of it. With a heavy head and little sleep, I left before sunrise, heading toward the road to catch a ride to Isilkul.

That summer, I visited the Enchanted Lake four more times, at different times of the day and in various weather conditions. By the end of the season, the bees were flourishing, flying in remarkable numbers, and bringing bright yellow pollen into their burrows. However, I couldn't say the same for myself. Just a meter from the cliff, above their nests, I continued to experience the same disturbing sensations, yet five meters away, all was calm.

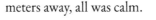

The Revelation of the Miracle

Years later, I discovered the reason when the bee city in the Kamyshlov Valley was destroyed: the plowing had reached the cliff, causing it to collapse. Where once there had been life, now only a massive, unsightly dump remained. I salvaged a few old clay clumps—remnants of the nests—each filled with small chambers. These chambers were arranged side by side, resembling tiny thimbles or small jugs with gently narrowing necks. I already knew that these bees were of the species *Halictus quadricinctus*—the "four-banded halictid bee," named for the four light rings on their elongated abdomens.

On my work table, cluttered with instruments, ant farms, grasshoppers, vials of chemicals, and other assorted items, sat a wide dish filled with the porous clay clumps from the bees' nests. As I reached over the dish to grab something, a peculiar sensation struck me—a distinct warmth radiated above the clumps. Surprised, I touched the clay fragments, only to find them cold to the touch. Yet, above them, I felt a warmth, along with strange pulses, twitches, and "ticks" in my fingers.

Curious, I moved the dish to the edge of the table and leaned in closer, bringing my face over it. Instantly, the same sensations I had experienced at the lake returned: a feeling of my head becoming light and large, my body sinking somewhere, sparks flickering in my eyes, that metallic battery taste in my mouth, and a slight wave of nausea.

To test further, I placed a piece of cardboard over the dish—the sensations persisted unchanged. I then added a metal lid from a pot, but it made no difference. It was as if this "something" pierced right through the barrier.

Realizing the urgency of studying this phenomenon, I attempted to investigate it at home, though I lacked proper physical instruments. Colleagues from various institutes in our town helped me examine the nests. Unfortunately, despite our best efforts, the instruments—whether thermometers, ultrasound recorders, electrometers, or magnetometers—detected nothing unusual. Even a thorough chemical analysis of the clay revealed nothing out of the ordinary, and the radiometer remained silent.

However, ordinary human hands—mine and others—clearly felt warmth, or a cold breeze, or tingling, or twitches, or a denser, jelly-like medium over the nests; for some, their hand felt heavier, for others, it seemed like something was pushing it upward; some people's fingers went numb, muscles in their forearm cramped, heads spun, and saliva flowed abundantly.

A similar effect was observed with a bundle of paper tubes completely filled with leaf-cutting bees. In each tunnel, there was a solid row of multi-layered cups made from leaf fragments, sealed with concave round lids—also made of leaves; inside the cups were silk oval cocoons with larvae and pupae. I asked people, who knew nothing about my discovery, to hold their hand or face over the leaf-cutter nests, and I documented everything in detail. The results of these unusual experiments can be found in my article "On the Physico-Biological Properties of Pollinator Bee Nests," published in the third issue of *Siberian Bulletin of Agricultural Science* in 1984. The article also includes the formula for the discovery—a brief physical explanation of this surprising phenomenon.

Building on my findings from the bee nests, I created several dozen artificial "honeycombs" from plastic, paper, metal, and wood, and it turned out that the cause of all these unusual sensations was not a "biofield" but the size, shape, number, and arrangement of cavities formed by any solid bodies. And still, the human body sensed it, while the instruments remained "silent."

I named the discovery the cavity structure effect—CSE—and continued and diversified the experiments, and Nature continued to reveal her hidden secrets to me, one after the other.

It turned out that in the zone of influence of CSE, the development of saprophytic soil bacteria, yeast, and other fungi was noticeably suppressed, wheat seeds' germination was affected, the behavior of microscopic mobile algae, chlamydomonas, changed, bee larvae began to glow, and adult bees behaved much more actively in this field, completing their pollination work two weeks earlier.

It turned out that CSE cannot be shielded, like gravity, and it acts on living things through walls, thick metal, and other barriers.

It turned out that if you move a honeycomb-like object to a new place, a person will not feel the CSE immediately, but after a few seconds or minutes, and at the old place, a "trace" remains, or as I jokingly called it, a "phantom," which can be felt by hand even tens of minutes, or sometimes months, later.

It turned out that the CSE field does not diminish evenly from the honeycombs but is surrounded by a whole system of invisible, but sometimes very clearly perceptible "shells."

It turned out that animals (white mice) and people who entered the zone of even a strong CSE gradually got used to it, adapted to it. This is not surprising, as we are surrounded by numerous large and small cavities, grids, cells—living and dead plants (including our own cells), foam, styrofoam, foamed concrete, rooms, corridors, halls, roofs, spaces between components of control panels, instruments, machines, between trees, furniture, buildings.

It turned out that the "beam" or "ray" of CSE affects living things more strongly when it is directed in the opposite direction of the sun, as well as downward, toward the center of the Earth.

It turned out that in a strong CSE field, clocks—both mechanical and electronic—sometimes "lie," suggesting that time itself might be involved.

It turned out that all of this is a manifestation of Matter Waves—ever-moving, ever-changing, and ever-existing. Physicist Louis de Broglie first discovered these waves, earning him the Nobel Prize in the 1920s, and today, these waves are fundamental in the operation of electron microscopes. This discovery opened up a vast and complex field, touching on solid-state physics, quantum mechanics, and particle physics. Yet, this is a story not just of waves and particles but of insects.

I managed to develop devices capable of objectively registering the cavity structure effect (CSE), which react remarkably to the proximity of insect nests. You can see one in the picture: a hermetically sealed container where straws and charred branches—drawing charcoal—are suspended on spider webs at an angle, with a bit of water at the bottom to eliminate static electricity that can interfere with experiments in dry air. When you bring an old wasp's nest, a honeycomb, or a bundle of wheat ears close to the top end of the indicator, it gradually moves away by several degrees. There's no magic here: the energy from the flickering electrons of these multi-cavity structures creates a system of summed waves in space. A wave is energy, and this energy can perform work by repelling objects from each other—even through barriers like thick-walled steel capsules.

It's almost unimaginable that waves from something as small and lightweight as a wasp's nest can penetrate such armor, yet the indicator inside the heavy, sealed capsule sometimes moves away from a long-abandoned wasp's nest by half a turn. But that's the reality. If you're skeptical, I invite you to visit the Agroecology Museum near Novosibirsk, where you can witness these phenomena firsthand.

At the Museum, there's a unique device I developed—a honeycomb pain reliever. It's simple: anyone who sits on a chair beneath a case containing several frames of empty but full-sized honeycomb (referred to as "dry" in beekeeping) will almost certainly feel something after a few minutes. If you experience anything—whatever it may be—I'd appreciate it if you wrote to me about it. Particularly for those suffering from headaches, the relief is often swift, providing at least a few hours of respite. These pain relievers have been successfully implemented in various locations across the country, and I've never kept this discovery a secret. The radiation emitted by the honeycombs is detectable by hand—simply hold your palm upward and bring it under the honeycomb case. The case itself can be made of cardboard, plywood, or, even better, tin, with tightly sealed seams.

This is yet another invaluable gift from the insect world.

The deep pits on an insect's exoskeleton, for instance, create a protective wave field—a crucial defense mechanism, especially for wasps that stealthily lay their eggs in the nests of other wasps and bees.

Initially, I thought about it this way: humans have interacted with honeybees for thousands of years, and aside from the occasional sting, no one has reported any negative effects from handling honeycombs. I tested it myself by holding a frame with dry comb over my head—it worked! I eventually settled on using a set of six frames. And that's the entire story behind this relatively simple yet effective discovery.

A wasp's nest, however, functions quite differently, despite the similar size and shape of its cells to those of honeycombs. The key differences lie in the material and structure: unlike the wax honeycombs of bees, the cells in a wasp's nest are made of a looser, microporous paper, which wasps invented long before humans—they scrape old wood fibers and mix them with their sticky saliva. The walls of these paper cells are much thinner than bee cells, the arrangement and size of the combs differ, and the nest also includes an outer shell made of several layers of paper, with gaps between them.

I've received several reports about the negative effects of wasp nests built in attics. Generally, most multi-cellular structures and objects with a pronounced Cavity Structure Effect (CSE) have less than beneficial impacts on people in the initial minutes or hours of exposure. Honeybee combs are among the few exceptions to this rule.

In the 1960s, when bumblebees made their home in our Isilkul apartment, I observed a fascinating phenomenon on more than one occasion. A young bumblebee, venturing out for the first time through a long tube from its hive to the entrance in the window frame, often struggled to remember its way back. It would wander around not only the windows of our house but also those of the neighboring, similar-looking house. By evening, exhausted and frustrated with its poor visual memory, the bumblebee would sit on the brick wall directly opposite its hive and attempt to "break through" the bricks as if it knew that just a few meters away and behind the wall lay its home. At the time, I was puzzled by this behavior, but now I realize it was likely due to a wave beacon created by the cavity of the hive—a discovery that continues to amaze me.

This phenomenon reminded me of the City of Pompils in the Nursery, where hunting wasps returned not only to a specific point in the area but also to a completely different spot where a clump of earth with a burrow had been moved. The wave beacon created by the nest cavity was undoubtedly guiding them back.

In those years, another secret was revealed to me by my insect friends, this time related to the flowers of plants. I discovered that flowers, besides attracting pollinators with their color, scent, and nectar, also emit a powerful wave beacon. This beacon, similar to the one I observed in insect nests, is unshielded and can be detected using a simple drawing charcoal stick—burnt twig—by moving it in front of large bell-shaped flowers like tulips, lilies, amaryllis, mallows, and pumpkins. Even from a distance, you could feel the "braking" effect of this "detector." With practice, I was almost always able to locate a flower in a dark room from one or two meters away, as long as it hadn't been moved—otherwise, a "residual phantom" lingered at the old spot.

This discovery isn't limited to those with special abilities; anyone can learn to sense it with some practice. You can use a piece of yellow broomstick stem or a short pencil with the blunt end pointing at the flower. Some might feel the "heat," "cold," or "tingles" from the flower with their palm, tongue, or even face. Numerous experiments have shown that children and teenagers are especially more sensitive than adults to these "flower" Matter Waves.

As for underground-nesting bees, "knowledge of CSE" is vital to them, first of all, so that when digging a new gallery, the builder doesn't break into a neighbor's nest but instead bypasses it from a distance. Otherwise, the entire bee city, riddled with intersecting burrows, would collapse. Secondly, plant roots—which, as we know, can break buildings—must not be allowed to grow into galleries and cells. And, stopping just a few centimeters short of the cells, the roots halt their growth or divert, sensing the proximity of bee nests. This was clearly confirmed in my numerous experiments on wheat seed germination in a strong CSE field compared to control seeds developed under the same temperature, humidity, and light conditions: the pictures and drawings show the death of roots in the experimental batch and their sharp deviation in the direction opposite my "artificial honeycombs."

It turned out that between the grasses and bees at the lake, there had long been this alliance—one of the examples of the highest ecological rationality of all Being; and there, in the same spot on the globe, another example of ruthless, ignorant human behavior toward Nature. The bee city is now completely gone, and every spring, thick streams of once-fertile black soil flow down between the filthy piles of garbage to the lifeless, steeply salty puddles, which were, not so long ago, a chain of lakes, over which countless flocks of sandpipers and ducks soared, bright white swans could be seen on the water, and predators hovered on broad wings. And by the cliff, riddled with bee burrows, there was a hum from hundreds of thousands of tireless wings of the halictids, which opened the first door to the Unknown for me.

I may have tired the reader with all my honeycombs, structures, and grids. It would take a separate thick book to describe all my experiments, so I'll just mention this. In the CSE field, my BZ18A pocket calculator, which ran on a battery, repeatedly malfunctioned: it either lied outrageously, or its display wouldn't light up for several hours. I affected it with a wasp's nest, supplemented with CSE from my two palms; individually, these structures didn't influence the calculator.

I should note that the hands, with their tubular phalanges, joints, ligaments, tendons, vessels, and nails, are intense CSE emitters. They can easily push the straw or charcoal indicator of my device from a couple of meters away. This effect works for everyone, which is why I'm convinced that there are no "psychics"—rather, everyone has some degree of telekinetic ability. Many more people than generally believed can move light objects across a table, hold them suspended in the air, or "magnetize" them to their hand from a distance in the same way. These feats, often shown on TV as miraculous, are within reach of anyone willing to try. I await your letters with your own experiences.

There was an old folk amusement: a person sits on a chair, and four of their friends "build" a grid over their head with horizontal palms with slightly spread fingers—first the right hands, then the left above, with gaps of about two centimeters between the palms. After ten or fifteen seconds, all four quickly insert their joined index and middle fingers under the seated person's knees and armpits and, on command, lift them energetically. The time between "dismantling" the grid and lifting should not exceed two seconds, and synchronization is crucial. In successful cases, a 220-pound person feels as light as a feather and is almost lifted to the ceiling.

In one of my experiments, the CSE emitter was not placed directly above the growing roots but to the side, and the roots sharply turned in the opposite direction.

How is this possible, the strict reader will ask, when all this contradicts the laws of nature, and Grebennikov preaches mysticism? Nothing of the sort—no mysticism here. We simply know very little about the Universe, which, as we see, doesn't always "acknowledge" our human rules, regulations, and commands.

One day, it dawned on me: the results of my experiments with insect nests are very similar to reports from people who have been near UFOs. Recall and compare: temporary malfunctioning of electronic devices, "tricks" with clocks—meaning time, an invisible elastic "barrier," temporary reduction in the weight of objects, the sensation of a person's weight decreasing, phosphenes—colorful moving "images" in the eyes, and a "galvanic" taste in the mouth. You've undoubtedly read about all these phenomena in UFO-related articles—and you can see and experience almost all of it in our Museum. Come visit!

Part Two

It felt like I was standing on the brink of another mystery, and indeed I was. Once again, luck—or perhaps my insect friends—guided me. This led to sleepless nights filled with failures, doubts, the struggle to gather missing materials, breakdowns, and even accidents. There was no one to turn to; anyone I told would laugh at me, or worse. But let me tell you, reader: happiness belongs to those whose eyes, mind, and hands work in harmony—hands that are skilled and capable. The joy of creation, even when it doesn't end in success, far surpasses the satisfaction of earning a diploma, a medal, or a patent.

Consider this excerpt from my work diaries, edited for this book, and therefore greatly simplified and shortened. The photos and drawings will help you grasp what's written.

It was a hot summer day. The horizon was shrouded in a bluish-purple haze, with a vast dome of sky above, filled with lush clouds that seemed to rest on an invisible pane of glass. The bottom of each cloud was flat and even, while their sunlit tops were so bright that they made me squint.

I was flying about three hundred meters above the ground, using a distant lake—a pale, elongated spot in the hazy distance—as my landmark. The blue thickets of bizarre shapes slowly receded beneath me; fields spread out between them: the bluish-green ones in the distance were oats; the whitish rectangles with a strange, shimmering glow were buckwheat; directly below me was an alfalfa field, its green closest in shade to the artist's "medium green cobalt"; and to the right, the denser green of wheat fields, resembling the color "chrome oxide." An enormous multicolored palette kept flowing past beneath me.

Between the fields and groves, winding paths converged into dirt roads, which in turn led to the highway, still hidden by the haze. But I knew that if I flew to the right of the lake, it would appear: a perfectly straight, light strip stretching endlessly in both directions, with tiny cars crawling along it.

The sunlit forest-steppe was scattered with the uneven, flat shadows of cumulus clouds, deep blue where they covered the groves, and on the fields, shades of blue. At that moment, I was in the shadow of one such cloud; I increased speed—easily—and flew out of the shadow.

Leaning slightly forward, I felt a warm, dense wind rising from below, heated by the earth and plants, not the usual side wind you'd feel on the ground, but an unusual upward wind. I could physically feel the thick, fragrant stream, rich with the scent of blooming buckwheat—a current strong enough to lift a large bird if it spread its wings motionless, like an eagle, crane, or stork.

But it wasn't the rising currents that held me aloft; I had no wings. In flight, I stood on a flat rectangular platform, slightly larger than a chair lid, with a stand and two handles that I used to control the device. Science fiction? Maybe.

The manuscript of this book lay untouched for two years because Nature, through my insect friends, again gave me something else to do—elegantly, unobtrusively, but swiftly and convincingly. For two long years, the Discovery wouldn't let me go, though I thought I was mastering it quickly. But that's how it always is: when something is truly interesting and new, time flies almost twice as fast.

The light spot of the steppe lake had drawn closer, growing larger, and beyond it, the highway came into view, with the tiny cars clearly distinguishable even from this height. The highway was about eight kilometers from the railway, which ran parallel to it. In the distance, I could see the supports of the catenary system and the light embankment of the railway track. It was time to turn about twenty degrees to the left.

I can't be seen from below, not just because of the altitude. Even during low flights, I rarely cast a shadow. Still, I later learned that people occasionally notice something unusual in the sky—sometimes a glowing sphere or disk, other times something like a vertical or oblique cloud with sharp edges, moving in a way they say "doesn't look like a cloud." One person even claimed to see a "flat, opaque square the size of a hectare"—perhaps they glimpsed an enlarged image of my platform? Most of the time, though, people don't see anything, and for now, that suits me just fine—especially since I still haven't figured out what controls this "visibility-invisibility." As a result, I've taken to avoiding people, flying well clear of

cities and villages, and crossing roads at high speed, only after ensuring they're deserted.

These excursions, which may seem fantastic to the reader, have become almost routine for me. My insect friends, who you'll see depicted on these pages, are my only companions. My latest discovery's first practical use, and still the primary one, is entomological—surveying my cherished natural spots from above, discovering new "Insect Lands" that need protection and preservation.

But nature has set strict limits, just as in passenger planes: you can look, but you can't photograph. In my case, it's worse—the shutter won't close, and the films I brought along, whether in the camera or in my pocket, were completely exposed. Sketching the terrain from up high didn't work either; my hands are almost always occupied, and I can only free one for a few seconds. So I'm left to rely on my memory, which isn't great, even as an artist.

This flight is nothing like what we experience in dreams, and it's not so much a pleasure as it is hard work—sometimes very difficult and unsafe. You don't soar; you stand. Your hands are always busy, and just a few centimeters away is the boundary between "this" space and "that" external one—a boundary that's invisible but treacherous. My creation might remind someone of hospital scales, but this is just the beginning.

Incidentally, my watch often malfunctions, and possibly the calendar too. Sometimes, when descending to a familiar clearing, I find it slightly out of season, with a "deviation" of about a week in either direction, and nothing to compare it to. So, it seems possible to move not only through space but also, perhaps, through time. I can't confirm this with complete certainty, but during the flight—especially at the start—my watch alternates between speeding up and slowing down, only to keep perfect time by the end of the journey. That's why I avoid people during these excursions—if time and gravity are at play, what if it disrupts some unknown cause-and-effect relationships, and someone suffers as a result?

My insect companions, taken "there" in test tubes or containers, often disappear without a trace. Once, a test tube shattered into tiny fragments in my pocket; another time, an oval hole with seemingly "chitinous" edges appeared in the glass. Occasionally, I've felt a brief burning or electric shock through my pocket fabric, probably at the moment a captive insect "disappeared." Only once did I find the insect I had taken in a test tube, but it wasn't the adult ichneumon wasp I had captured—it was its pupa, still alive, wiggling its abdomen when touched. Sadly, it died and dried up within a week.

The best flights—no quotes needed—are on clear summer days. Rain hinders the process, and for some reason, winter flights are impossible. Not because of the cold—I could adapt the device if needed—but as an entomologist, winter flights simply aren't necessary.

How and why did I come to this discovery?

In the summer of 1988, while studying the intricate details of insect anatomy, I stumbled upon something extraordinary. Among the various exoskeletons, antennae, and wing structures I examined, one particular insect detail caught my attention. It was an incredibly rhythmic and highly ordered microstructure, as if crafted by a precise machine. This unique pattern, located on the lower part of an insect's elytra, was unlike anything I had seen in nature or technology. What made it even more puzzling was that this elaborate design seemed unnecessary for the insect's survival or appearance—especially since it was almost always hidden from view.

Intrigued by the possibility that these structures might serve a purpose beyond the ordinary, such as receiving or generating electronic waves or even counteracting Earth's gravity, I decided to investigate further. That summer, I was fortunate enough to find many specimens of this insect, and I began collecting them by the light of the evening. I placed one of these chitinous plates under a microscope and admired its intricate design. On a whim, I placed another identical plate on top of the first one, using tweezers.

To my astonishment, the plate escaped the tweezers, hovered in the air, rotated slightly, moved to the right, turned again, swayed, and then fell onto the table. It was as if the plate had a mind of its own. Shocked but determined, I tied several of these plates together to form a multi-layered "chitin block." Placing it on the table, I noticed that even a heavy object like a large pushpin couldn't fall onto it; instead, the pushpin was deflected upward and to the side. When I attached the pushpin to the top of the "block," unimaginable things began to happen—at one point, the pushpin even disappeared from sight!

This discovery was not a mere beacon as I had initially suspected, but something far more profound. The implications of what I had found were overwhelming, and I knew that this was just the beginning. I still needed to rethink, test, and verify everything. My work was far from over, and I promised myself that I would eventually share the full details of my device, its operation, and the principles behind its movement. But that would have to wait for my next book.

One of the most harrowing flights took place on the night of March 17 to 18, 1990—a risky venture undertaken too soon and in the dead of night, which I already knew was the most dangerous time for such work.

The misfortunes began even before takeoff: the block panels on the right side of the supporting platform were jamming—a problem I should have fixed immediately, but didn't. I recklessly took off directly from the street in our Vaskhnil town, assuming that at two in the morning, everyone would be asleep and no one would see me. The ascent initially seemed normal, but within a few seconds, as the houses with their rare lit windows fell below and I reached about a hundred meters above the ground, I felt faint, as if I were about to lose consciousness. I should have descended immediately, but I didn't. That was my mistake because suddenly, some powerful force seemed to wrest control of movement and weight away from me, pulling me relentlessly towards the city.

Dragged by this unexpected, uncontrollable force, I crossed the second circle of nine-story buildings in the residential area of the town (arranged in two huge circles, each a kilometer in diameter, with five-story buildings inside, including ours), flew over a snowy narrow field, and diagonally crossed the Novosibirsk-Akademgorodok highway and the Severo-Chemsky residential area. The dark mass of Novosibirsk was rapidly approaching—along with several clusters of tall factory chimneys, many of which were slowly and thickly smoking from the night shift. Something needed to be done urgently.

With great difficulty, I managed to regain control, performing an emergency readjustment of the block panels. The horizontal movement began to slow, but I felt faint again—completely unacceptable during flight. It took four attempts to stop the horizontal movement and hover over Zatulinka, the industrial Kirovsky district of the city. The ominous chimneys continued to silently and steeply smoke very close beneath me. After resting for a few minutes—if one can call it rest, hovering above a lit factory fence, with residential quarters beginning immediately nearby—and realizing with relief that the "evil force" had disappeared, I glided back. But instead of heading straight for Vaskhnil town, I veered right towards Tolmachevo, to confuse any potential observers. About halfway to the airport, over some dark, empty fields, I sharply turned home...

The next day, I could barely get out of bed. The news reports on television and in the newspapers were more than alarming. Headlines like "UFO Over Zatulinka" and "Aliens Again?" clearly indicated that my flight had been detected. But how! Some witnesses described the "phenomenon" as glowing spheres or disks, with many inexplicably claiming to have seen not one sphere but two! It's true what they say: fear makes the eyes see things. Others reported seeing "a real saucer" with portholes and beams.

I don't discount the possibility that some people in Zatulinka witnessed something entirely different, unrelated to my near-crash maneuvers. Especially since March 1990 was an unusually active month for UFO sightings in Siberia, near Nalchik, and notably in Belgium. On the night of March 31, as reported by the newspaper Pravda, engineer Marcel Alferlain, armed with a video camera, climbed onto his roof and captured a two-minute video of one of the massive "alien" triangular gravitoplanes, which, according to the authoritative conclusion of Belgian scientists, were "material objects with capabilities beyond what any known civilization could currently create."

Is that so, Belgian scientists? I would suggest that the gravitational platform-filters (or as I call them, block panels) of these devices were relatively small, triangular in shape, and very much made here on Earth, though on a more solid and sophisticated basis than my almost half-wooden device. Initially, I intended to make my platform triangular—it's more efficient and reliable—but I opted for a quadrangular shape because it's easier to fold. When folded, it resembles a briefcase, an easel, or a "diplomat," which can be disguised so as not to arouse the slightest suspicion. Naturally, I chose the "easel"...

As for the events in Belgium and near Nalchik, I had no involvement. In fact, I use my discovery in ways that might seem almost foolish to others—merely to visit my "entomo-parks"...These parks, which I consider far more significant than any technical achievement, now number eleven: eight in the Omsk region, one in the Voronezh region, and two in the Novosibirsk region. Six of them near Novosibirsk were created—or rather, saved—by my hands and the hands of my family. Unfortunately, this work is not well-regarded here—neither at our agricultural academy, where they still favor chemistry, nor in the nature protection society or the nature protection committee. Despite my pleas, they have shown little interest in preserving these small insect reserves and sanctuaries from destruction by malicious or short-sighted people.

And so, I continue my journey under majestic clouds, heading west. The rectangular patches of multicolored fields, the groves of bizarre shapes, and the blue shadows from the clouds steadily recede behind me. The flight speed is quite high, yet the wind doesn't whistle in my ears. The force field created by the platform's block panels "cuts out" an upward invisible column or beam, severing the platform's connection to Earth's gravity—but not mine, nor the air within this column. As I fly, it feels as though space itself is expanding, only to snap shut behind me. This might explain why the device, along with its "rider"—or more accurately, its "stander"—becomes invisible or partially distorted, as happened to me recently over Novosibirsk's Zatulinka. The gravity protection is adjustable, though not perfect: if I lean forward, I can feel eddies from the oncoming wind, carrying the distinct smells of sweet clover, buckwheat, or the mixed fragrance of Siberian meadow grasses.

Isilkul, with its towering grain elevator by the railway, lay far to my left as I began my gradual descent over the highway. I made sure to remain invisible to the drivers, passengers, and workers in the fields below. Neither I nor the platform cast a shadow on the ground—though occasionally, a shadow would unexpectedly appear. Nearby, on the edge of a grove, I spotted three boys picking berries. I slowed down, flying low over them. Everything appeared normal; no reaction from the boys, confirming that neither I nor my shadow was visible. And of course, there was no sound—this method of travel, using "expanded space," eliminates air friction, making the device utterly silent.

The journey had been long—no less than forty minutes from Novosibirsk. My hands, which couldn't leave the controls, were tired, as were my legs and body. I had to stand almost at attention on this small platform, strapped in with a belt. Though I could travel faster, I hesitated; my "technique," made in a semi-artisan manner, was still too small and fragile.

Up again and straight ahead; soon, familiar landmarks came into view: a road intersection, a passenger pavilion to the right of the highway. After another five kilometers, I finally saw the orange posts marking the Sanctuary's fence—a place that, incredibly, had just turned twenty years old.

I had saved this first creation of mine from numerous disasters and bureaucrats, from planes spraying chemicals, from fires, and many other threats. And now this Insect Land was alive, flourishing! As I descended and slowed down, adjusting the louver-filters beneath the platform, I could already see the lush thickets of carrot plants, their delicate lace-like inflorescences swarming with insects. A profound joy filled my soul, completely relieving my fatigue: I had preserved this small piece of Earth, less than seven hectares, for twenty whole years. No plowing, no mowing, no grazing—the soil layer had risen in places to fourteen centimeters. Endangered species of insects had reappeared, along with grasses that had once vanished from the area, like rare feather grass and purple scorzonera, whose large flowers smell like chocolate in the mornings, among many other plants.

The steep "adonis-carrot" scent, unique to this Middle Glade just beyond the Sanctuary's fence, fills me with renewed joy at the prospect of reuniting with the Insect World. Even from ten meters above, I can easily spot the dark orange fritillary butterflies clustered on the sprawling umbrellas and lace spheres of angelica and carrot plants. Large bronze beetles weigh down the white and yellow blossoms of bedstraw, while reddish and blue dragonflies hover at my level, their broad wings glistening in the sunlight. I slow my descent, but suddenly, there's a dark flash below—my shadow, previously invisible, now slides slowly across the grass and bushes. But there's no need to worry; there's no one around, and the highway, three hundred meters north of the Sanctuary, is clear of cars. I can safely land. The tallest grasses already rustle against my platform, signaling the moment to set down.

As I approach the north edge of the Sanctuary in 1991, the uncut meadow grasses are in full bloom beyond the fence. Deep within this forest lies the secluded spot where my gravitoplane takes off and lands. If you rise half a kilometer above the Sanctuary on a clear day, you can see it all: fields, groves, villages, roads, clouds and their shadows, birds... In the distance, the Yunino siding is visible, and beyond that, the northern Kazakh steppes fade into a blue haze.

But before setting down on this hill, overcome with joy, I adjust the louver panels with a lever and shoot vertically upward like a rocket. The scene below rapidly contracts—the groves of the Sanctuary, its edges, and fence, the surrounding fields and groves. The horizon begins to curve outward, revealing the railway two kilometers to the left and the villages to the right. Beyond the highway, Rosslavka gleams with its light slate roofs. Further right lies the central estate of the "Lesnoy" state farm, already resembling a small town. To the left of the railway, cattle farms of the Komsomol division of the "Lesnoy" state farm are encircled by a wide yellow ring of straw and trampled manure. Far to the west, where the railway's smooth arc curves away, I spot small houses and the white cube of the neat station building at the Yunino siding, six kilometers from the Sanctuary. Beyond Yunino stretch the boundless expanses of Kazakhstan, melting into the blue sultry haze.

And now, all of Isilkulya, the land of my youth, unfolds beneath me—not as on maps or plans with their inscriptions and symbols, but as a boundless, living landscape. The dark, whimsical islands of groves, the shifting shadows of clouds, the bright clear spots of lakes, all spread out across the vast disk of the Earth. For some reason, this familiar view always appears more and more concave—a long-standing illusion I have yet to understand.

I climb higher and higher, leaving the rare white masses of cumulus clouds below. The sky is no longer the familiar blue of the ground, but a deep, almost indigo hue. The groves and fields, once so vivid between the clouds, now blur into a thickening blue haze, becoming harder to distinguish. I catch sight of a glory—a bright rainbow ring—on a cloud below.

How I wish I could share this experience with my grandson, Andryusha. He's only four years old, and the platform could easily lift us both. But the risk is too great—who knows what might happen?

Suddenly, I realize the danger: down there on the Glade, I was casting a shadow—people might see me. Unlike that ill-fated March night, it's daytime now, and I could be visible to thousands, not just a few. Worse still, a plane is approaching—silent for now, but rapidly growing in size. I can already see the cold gleam of its duralumin body, the pulsation of its unnaturally red beacon. I quickly descend, braking sharply and turning to put the Sun at my back. I search for my shadow on the giant convex wall of a dazzling white cumulus cloud, but it's not there. Instead, I see only a multicolored glory—my heart eases: no shadow means no one saw me, nor my "double" as a triangle, square, or "mundane" saucer.

A thought flashes through my mind (and I must say, despite the desperate technical and physical challenges, my imagination works much better and faster in a "falling" flight): What if I'm not the only one who has made this discovery? What if others, somewhere among the five billion people on Earth, have created flying devices based on the same principles? Perhaps these shielding platforms, whether crafted in factory design bureaus or homemade like mine, share a common property: they sometimes become visible to others in various forms. The pilots, too, might "transform," appearing as "humanoids" in silver suits, sometimes small and green, sometimes flat like cardboard (as in Voronezh, 1989), or something else entirely. It could very well be that these aren't aliens or UFOnauts at all, but rather "temporarily/visually deformed"—of course, only for outside observers—earthly pilots and designers, refining their creations.

For those who, while studying insects, happen upon this phenomenon and begin constructing or testing a "gravitoplane," let me offer some essential advice. Firstly, fly only on clear, fine summer days; avoid thunderstorms, rain, or any adverse weather conditions. Keep your altitude and distance modest; don't venture too high or too far. Take nothing from the landing site with you, and ensure that every component of your device is as robust as possible.

During tests and flights, stay far from power lines, settlements, cities, transportation routes, or any gatherings of people. Ideally, choose a remote, secluded forest clearing far from human habitation. Otherwise, within a radius of several dozen meters, you may unintentionally trigger what is commonly called a poltergeist—unexplainable movements of household objects, sudden disconnection or activation of electrical appliances, or even fires. Although I can't fully explain this, it seems these events are related to time distortions, which are unpredictable and dangerous.

Be cautious not to drop or lose any part of your device, no matter how small, during flight or at the landing site. This is critical. Remember the "Dalnegorsk phenomenon" of January 29, 1986, where an entire apparatus was destroyed and scattered over a large area, leaving only fragments that defied chemical analysis. It's possible that some UFO sightings are actually descriptions of platforms, panels, or other components from such devices, deliberately or accidentally ejected from their active fields by designers or experimenters. These fragments can cause serious harm or, at the very least, generate a plethora of bizarre stories and dubious "scientific" explanations in the media.

Finally, consider the mysterious holes that appear in glass—often seen in residential or office buildings. These holes, which can appear in a series across multiple windows and floors, seem to be linked to the testing or flights of devices like mine. They resemble the holes I observed when transporting insects in test tubes during my experiments. It's crucial to be meticulous and avoid careless handling of materials during your work.

Part Three

Why am I not revealing the core of my discovery right now? First, because proving it requires time and energy—resources I currently lack. My previous attempts to gain recognition for my findings, like the cavity structure effect, have taught me that the scientific community is often resistant to new ideas. Despite years of effort to prove the existence of this phenomenon, I was ultimately met with dismissal. I've seen how the Gatekeepers of Science react—skeptical to the point of rejection, even if I were to demonstrate my device in front of them, flying it right before their eyes. The result would likely be indifference, or worse, they might dismiss it outright as a magic trick.

To you, young people, who will one day replace these Gatekeepers—embrace the future with open minds!

The second reason for my secrecy is more practical. I discovered these anti-gravitational structures in a single species of Siberian insect, a species that might be on the brink of extinction. I'm reluctant to even reveal its order, let alone its genus or species, because the risk of unscrupulous individuals exploiting this knowledge is too high. If word got out, who's to say that these insects wouldn't be hunted to the brink, their habitats destroyed in the pursuit of a lucrative prize?

So, for those with dishonest intentions, let everything I've written here remain science fiction. Nature guards its secrets fiercely, revealing them only to those who have earned them. Even if you dedicate your life to studying every insect species, the chances of stumbling upon something as extraordinary as what I've found are slim. It would take a thousand years, with unwavering diligence, perfect vision, and memory, to study just a fraction of the millions of insect species on this planet. I can only wish you the best of luck and perhaps a bit of envy for the journey ahead.

I hope those who wish to familiarize themselves with my Discovery out of pure curiosity and with good intentions will understand my hesitation: How can I act otherwise to protect Living Nature? Especially when I observe that others, too, seem to have developed something similar, yet choose not to reveal their discoveries to bureaucratic offices, opting instead to fly in the night skies as enigmatic disks, triangles, or squares, shimmering and leaving passersby in awe.

Quickly descending—or rather, falling—I assess my surroundings to ensure no one is nearby. At about forty meters from the ground, I brake sharply and land smoothly in my usual spot: a tiny clearing in the Big Forest of the Nature Reserve. You'll find this spot on the map sketch, and later, if you visit, you'll see it in person. Don't judge me for the fact that some aspen branches appear cut or "struck by lightning"; precise vertical takeoffs and landings are difficult, and the initial trajectory is often slanted, especially during takeoff when, for some reason, the platform tends to veer in the opposite direction of the Sun, or sometimes the other way around.

After loosening the wing nuts on the control stand, I shorten it like an antenna on a portable radio, detach it from the platform, and fold the platform in half on its hinges. Now, it resembles an easel box, though slightly thicker. I place the "easel" in my backpack along with some food and a few tools for fence repairs, then weave my way through the aspens and low rosehip bushes toward the Central Glade.

 Before even leaving the forest, I encounter a good omen: a family of bright red fly agaric mushrooms arranged in a wide arc on the forest floor, forming what's traditionally called a "fairy's ring." But why must this beautiful mushroom, a hallmark of Siberian forests, be broken, kicked, or trampled? I've often asked mushroom pickers why they do this, and the answer is always the same: "Because you can't eat it!" Yet many things in the forest are inedible—turf, clay, sticks, stumps, stones. If bricks were scattered in the forest instead of fly agarics, no one would kick them. It seems these mushrooms are targeted simply because they're alive, destroyed for the sake of destruction. This raises a troubling thought: Do humans have an instinct to kick a mushroom, crush a bug, or shoot a bird, a rabbit, or even each other? Is this where rudeness, sadism, pogroms, and wars originate? I don't want to believe it, **but if I were an alien visiting Earth, observing how people mistreat living things, I'd turn my starship around and leave, postponing my next visit for at least five hundred Earth years.**

And how would you act, reader, if you were in the alien's place? Fortunately, this family of fly agarics is hidden from the gaze of ill-intentioned eyes and cruel feet, and every summer they bring me joy with their vibrant, vermilion-red caps, moist and speckled with whitish scales. But now, I have arrived at the Glade.

I step onto this untouched piece of Earth, as always, with a trembling heart. There's the eternal longing for my native Isilkul, so far from Novosibirsk, the fear that some "owner" might come and plow it, and the joy that it remains unplowed, unmowed, and untrodden.

It doesn't matter that in my backpack, disguised as an easel, I carry a folded and neutralized platform with gravity micro-mesh block filters, along with a stand equipped with field regulators and a strap to secure myself. Suppose I've leaped fifty years ahead with this discovery—what difference does it make? Eventually, people will master this and many other mysteries of Matter, Space, Gravity, and Time. But no supercivilization in any part of the Supergalaxy could ever recreate this Glade, with its complex, fragile, and trembling Life—its bedstraws, meadowsweets, and feather grasses, its orange-patched fritillaries, and the leisurely zygaenid moths, whose indescribably solemn color displays a pattern of crimson-red spots on a deep blue, shimmering background.

Where else in the Universe will there be a lilac-blue bellflower, where in its semi-transparent, mysterious depths, two spotted-wing flies perform their love dance, waving their transparent wings adorned with an elegant black-and-white stripe?

And on what other planet will a nearly tame lycaenid butterfly land on an outstretched palm to taste a salty treat—be it fat, sausage, or cheese—or simply stroll around, opening and closing its satin-gray wings with a turquoise tint, displaying the delicate pattern of round eye-spots on their underside?

Not so long ago, we humans began to fly: first in hot air balloons, then in airplanes; today, powerful rockets carry us to other celestial bodies. And tomorrow? Tomorrow, we may fly to other stars at near the speed of light, yet even the neighboring galaxy—the Andromeda Nebula—will still be out of reach.

But Humanity—if it earns the title of Rational!—will solve many of the Universe's mysteries and even surpass this limit. When that day comes, any worlds in the far corners of the Universe, trillions of light-years from Earth, will become almost instantly accessible.

However, this Glade, with its fritillaries, zygaenids, lycaenids, bronze beetles, and spotted-wing flies, may not remain unless I—since no one else can be relied on for now—manage to preserve it for future generations. So, what is more valuable for Humanity at this moment: this protected insect sanctuary, or my homemade, backpacked device, capable of developing a zenith thrust much less than a centner, and horizontal speeds of thirty to forty kilometers per second?

This is addressed to you, reader. But think carefully before giving a wise and serious answer. Look at these pictures—this is what this rather simple thing looks like in working and assembled form. The flexible cable inside the control handle transmits movement to the gravity louvers, allowing me to ascend or descend. Once, during a quick descent in free-fall mode, the left handle came off. I could have gone to the "better world," but not only did I not crash, I didn't even feel a jolt—just darkness as the platform dug a deep well in the plowland. Thankfully, it didn't land on the road, where it would have caused a lot of talk or, worse, attracted overly enthusiastic investigators.

Similar wells—without mounds and veering sideways—also appeared unexpectedly in the fields of the Khvorostyansk district of the Kuibyshev region on October 24, 1989. This event was detailed in "Komsomolskaya Pravda" on December 6 of that year. It turns out, I'm not alone in this experience. It seems I'm "reinventing the wheel."

Indeed, the top part of my device is somewhat "bicycle-like." The right handle controls horizontal

movement, achieved by tilting both groups of "elytra" louvers, also through a cable. I don't dare to go faster than 25 kilometers per minute, preferring to fly at one-tenth of that speed.

I don't know if I've convinced you, reader, that this technology will be accessible to practically everyone very soon. But I fear that Living Nature, if not urgently saved, will soon be inaccessible to anyone due to its complete absence.

However, I don't want to appear as a total miser in your eyes. So, I offer researchers another Patent of Nature, also related to Motion and Gravity. Physicists claim that creating a reactionless drive is impossible—that an apparatus completely isolated from its surrounding environment won't fly or move. But this exception is worth considering.

In 1981 near Novosibirsk, while studying the entomofauna of alfalfa—its pollinators and pests—I discovered something intriguing. Walking through the field, I swept the alfalfa with quick movements of my net, then dumped the contents—insects, leaves, and flowers—into a dark box attached to a glass jar. Such was the harsh method of studying insect species composition in the fields. Alas, this was my job, for which I received a salary at the Institute of Agriculture and Chemicalization of Agriculture.

I was just about to slam the lid of the mortuary and throw in a cotton ball with ether when...a light cocoon popped out. It was oval, seemingly dense, and opaque. Surely one of the captives accidentally pushed it into the mortuary; the cocoon itself couldn't jump, right?

But then, defying my doubts, the cocoon jumped again, hitting the glass wall before falling to the bottom.

I had to sacrifice the catch—the terrified insects eagerly fled to freedom. Isolating the strange cocoon, I placed it in a separate test tube. At home, I examined it under a binocular microscope—nothing special, just a cocoon like any other; three millimeters long, slightly over a millimeter wide. The walls were sturdy, as they should be.

The cocoon jumped energetically when exposed to—or perhaps warmed by—the sun; in the shade, it calmed down. Its jumps reached up to thirty millimeters in length and, even more remarkably, fifty millimeters in height! As far as I could tell, the cocoon flew almost without tumbling, smoothly;

however, high-speed filming would be needed to confirm this. Undoubtedly, some mechanical movement was being transmitted to the cocoon from inside by the larva or pupa of the insect. But how this happened was impossible to see.

To skip ahead, the cocoon eventually produced an ichneumon wasp from the family Ichneumonidae, specifically the species *Bathyplectes anurus*, which is useful because its larvae parasitize the alfalfa pest *Phytonomus variabilis*. The "flying" cocoon was supposed to eventually find a cool refuge—like a crack in the ground; it probably ended up in my net during one of its jumps.

All of this strongly resembled a poltergeist—the inexplicable "jumps" of household objects often described in print. I placed the cocoon on glass and watched carefully from below: could the larva somehow pull in the bottom of the cocoon before a jump and then release it suddenly? But nothing like that happened—the cocoon didn't dent, yet it still jumped high, no matter how I rolled it; even more remarkably, from a horizontal and slippery surface, it took off not vertically, but at an angle! I measured the trajectories: they reached up to 35 millimeters in length, almost 50 millimeters in height—meaning the cocoon leaped to a height thirty times its thickness!

I wondered, could this "flying capsule" be deprived of its support, so it wasn't resting on anything? But how? By placing it on a layer of loose cotton! I carefully teased apart a tuft of cotton—creating a cloud with fuzzy, indistinct edges. I gently placed the cocoon on the "cloud," set it out in the sun, and waited impatiently: if the insect inside the cocoon struck its bottom, causing it to rebound from the support, that impact should now be absorbed by the fine springy fibers of the cotton, and theoretically, the cocoon wouldn't budge.

But no: suddenly, my little cocoon sprang up and flew rapidly from the untouched cotton, "as expected"—upward and sideways. I measured the jump length—forty-two millimeters, so it was within the normal range. The insect was probably making its strike or impact not on the bottom, but on the top part of the cocoon, or in any case doing something up there that propelled the capsule.

To be honest, this excites me now; back in '81, I didn't see anything supernatural in my captive's jumps because I wasn't aware that reactionless drives, according to physics, don't exist and can't exist. Otherwise, I would have bred a hundred or two of these little wasps, since they turned out to be quite common, and thoroughly investigated everything.

But now let's fantasize a bit: what if *Bathyplectes* wanted to leave Earth altogether? An adult, winged insect couldn't do it because of the "ceiling"—our atmosphere is too thin at the top for winged creatures—but it's a different story for the larva in the cocoon. It lifts its capsule in a jump by five centimeters, and at the peak of the jump, it gives it another push the same way, and again, and again. If the cocoon were airtight—meaning enough air for the pilot's breathing—what would stop the capsule from leaving the atmosphere and continuing to build speed infinitely? Nothing!

That's the enticing, incredible value of reactionless drives, a concept often dismissed as pure fantasy. It's difficult even for a non-physicist to grasp: how can a tiny larva inside a cocoon cause it to leap five centimeters into the air? It seems impossible, yet it happens.

Another example is *Phaneus splendidulus* from Patagonia—a beetle that's just as remarkable. Physicists argue that this is "beyond the sciences" because it "contradicts the laws of nature." But *Bathyplectes anurus* doesn't know that, nor did the expert biologists who straightforwardly noted on page 26 of the academic guide to insects of the European part of the USSR (volume III, part Z): "The cocoon jumps as a result of sudden movements of the larva inside the cocoon."

So here's a functioning, tested example of a reliable reactionless drive. I present it to you, reader: breed these wasps, invent, design, build—and bon voyage! But time is of the essence. The alfalfa weevil, Phytonomus variabilis, is under heavy chemical attack, and while humanity might succeed in eradicating this pest, the price is steep. The ichneumon wasp Bathyplectes anurus, which only parasitizes this specific weevil, would vanish from the planet's fauna without its host.

The weevil Phytonomus, barely five millimeters long under the microscope, is the sole target for this peculiar wasp. Yet, it's being ruthlessly wiped out with poisons, and with it, perhaps, the wasp that defies physics with its mysterious, gravity-defying cocoon.

And yet, proposals for biological methods of pest control in Siberian fields—using wasps like Bathyplectes and other beneficial entomophages—continue to be categorically rejected by the leaders of Russian agriculture and the Russian Academy of Agricultural Sciences. I've spent two decades fighting this battle, and success remains as elusive as ever, much like Don Quixote tilting at windmills. It's not hard to see why: no one is going to shut down expensive chemical plants! And what do the Agrarians care about a reactionless drive if it threatens their ability to spray alfalfa with poison?

So, hurry, biologists, engineers, physicists! If Chemistry prevails, this Secret—and the entire chain of related Secrets—will be lost to humanity forever. And I assure you, this invention won't be replicated without the help of insects.

Believe me, I speak as an entomologist with 60 years of field experience.

At the end of my first book, *A Million Mysteries*, published in Novosibirsk in 1968, there's a drawing: a person flying over Akademgorodok, aided by a device composed of large insect wings. Back then, it was just a dream—a fantasy. But, strangely enough, this dream is coming true, not through blindly copying visible components like those insect wings—which now make me smile—but through a deeper study of living Nature. Without my friendship with insects, none of this would have been possible. And I'm convinced that others won't achieve anything without them, either.

So, preserve this world—the ancient, fascinating World of Insects. It is an infinite and unique treasury of the Secrets of the Universe.

I implore everyone to protect it.

As described in his book, Viktor Grebennikov's claims about a flying machine powered by an undisclosed microstructure could align with creative interpretations of quantum mechanics that are inspired by Plato, or be related to an entirely unknown physics and theory of nature. While Grebennikov's claims remain unverified, one could theorize that the mechanisms Grebennikov describes might involve manipulating fundamental properties of quantum systems.

We start with the idea that time (T) is not a standalone dimension but rather a measure of entropy—the natural progression of systems from order to disorder. In this context, time can be understood as an emergent property tied to entropy, expressed as T = S, where S represents entropy. If we imagine that matter at the quantum level is composed of fundamental triangular structures, the connections between these triangles—and thus the fabric of matter itself—might be disrupted or manipulated by understanding and interfering with the progression of entropy.

The modified equation that expresses this interaction might look something like this: $E = \frac{hc}{T}$

Here, E represents energy, $\hbar$ is the Planck constant, c is the speed of light, and T represents time as a function of entropy. In this equation, the manipulation of entropy (T) could theoretically interfere with the progression of time itself and thus the gravitational force within a closed system, potentially allowing for the kind of anti-gravity effects Grebennikov described.

This equation can be better understood when considered alongside fundamental quantum principles, such as those expressed in the Schrödinger equation: $i\hbar \frac{\partial \psi}{\partial t} = H^\wedge \psi$

In this equation, ψ represents the wave function of a quantum system, t represents the progression of time, and $\hat{H}$ (H-hat) is the Hamiltonian operator, symbolizing the total energy of the system. By extending this framework, one might theorize that manipulating the entropy (T) within a quantum system could alter the Hamiltonian, and thus the energy and time evolution of the system.

One way to understand quantum geometry is to think of the most basic unit of matter as a line that extends along a Plank length, which is the length that the speed of light traverses within a Plank second. These lines can be thought of as the most fundamental units of space-time, forming the foundation of reality. When three quantum entities (like particles or waves) interact at the smallest scales, they naturally form connections that result in triangular configurations. As these triangular structures combine, they build up the fabric of space-time itself, with their geometry influencing the properties of the universe at both large and small scales. The intricate web of connected triangles forms the basis for the particles, forces, and interactions that govern our reality. By understanding and potentially manipulating these quantum triangles—along with other geometric forms they naturally coalesce into, such as tetrahedrons, polygons, and more complex polyhedra—one could theoretically influence the fundamental fabric of space-time at the atomic levels, allowing for quantum effects to emerge. This approach bypasses the need for the classical understanding of gravity as described by relativity. In this quantum framework, space-time is not curved by mass and energy but rather constructed by the intricate arrangement of these quantum triangles, which represent the most basic units of matter and energy. The connections between these, when time is viewed as an entropic state, might be responsible for what we perceive as gravitational force in such a system. In such a system, the future, past and present as we perceive it might be an illusion. In reality, time may be a construct of our perception, organizing events in a sequence to make sense of our experiences, even though at the most fundamental level, all events may exist simultaneously in a dimension where time itself does not exist: *only information. What we perceive as "now" and the passage of time that we experience may be related to the particular configuration of the information that we make sense of as "the universe", with differences in the amount or complexity of information possibly giving rise to varying experiences of time across different regions of space.*

By isolating a small region of information from the rest of the universe—through an understanding of quantum geometry, time as entropy, and the frequency or movement of quantum systems through Planck length and time—one could potentially exploit unique geometries and frequencies to "manipulate" the bonds with the external universe. This might result in the creation of a closed system where time could pass differently, and the gravitational force we typically experience on Earth would cease to exist within this isolated environment. However, it should be noted that this is merely fanciful speculation on my part. I am not a physicist. This is merely suggested here to provide an alternative viewpoint to explain a possible avenue as any further exploration of the physics involved should be approached with caution until Grebennikov's claim has been scientifically verified. Nonetheless, if his discovery holds true, it opens up intriguing possibilities that could provide an explanation for the ancient accounts of Abaris the Hyperborean. The story of Abaris flying across the world, once dismissed as myth or exaggeration by both ancient and modern commentators, might not be as far-fetched as previously believed.

Part 3: On The Lost Age of Man

"There is an abundance of evidence to suggest that the roots of civilization are far older than we are taught to believe. Myths and legends, dismissed by many as mere folklore, may well contain the memories of a lost race, an ancient civilization that once spanned the globe."

Colin Wilson

History teaches us that before the Sumerians, there were no civilizations. Primitive man hunted, gathered, and occasionally farmed, but did not create cities, systems of writing, science and so on. However, the Sumerians themselves, who were much closer to their past than we, over six thousand years removed from their beginnings, would have disagreed with modern academia's assessment, which pretentiously assumes we know more about their beginnings than they did.

According to their ancient texts, particularly the Sumerian King List, the earliest rulers were said to have reigned for tens of thousands of years. One account of their origins, left by a Chaldean priest Berosus, is below:

"[3] How the Chaldeans recorded their history, as recounted by Alexander Polyhistor; concerning their writings and their first kingdom.

This is what Berosus related in Book One, and in Book Two he described the kings, one by one. He mentions the period when Nabonassar was king but only records the kings' names without detailing their deeds, perhaps because he didn't think they accomplished anything noteworthy—beyond listing their names. This is how he begins. Apollodorus says that Alorus was the first Chaldean king to rule in Babylon, reigning for 36,000 years. He states that the Chaldean ancients measured periods of years in this way. After stating this, he lists the kings of the Assyrians, one by one. There were 10 kings from the first king, Alorus, to Xisuthrus. He notes that during Xisuthrus's reign, the first great flood occurred, which Moses also mentions. He states that the reigns of these kings totaled 432,000 years, which equals 2043 myriad years in our terms. He describes them one by one as follows:

He says that after the death of Alorus, his son Alaparus ruled for 10,800 years; after Alaparus, the Chaldean Almelon, from the city of Pautibiblon (perhaps Bad-tibira), ruled for 46,800 years; after Almelon, Ammenon, from the city of Pautibiblon, ruled for 43,200 years. During his time, a creature named Idotion, with the composite form of a man and a fish, emerged from the Red Sea. After Ammenon, Amegalarus, from the city of Pautibiblon, ruled for 64,800 years, and after him, the shepherd Daonus, from the city of Pautibiblon, ruled for 36,000 years. During his time, four hybrid beings of the same man-fish type as Idotion once again emerged from the Red Sea. Then Edovanchus, from the city of Pautibiblon, ruled for 64,800 years. During his reign, another similar man-fish being called Odacon emerged from the Red Sea. He says that all of them were descended from Oannes, and he briefly describes them one by one. Then the Chaldean Amempsinus, from the city of Lanchara, ruled for 36,000 years. Then the Chaldean Otiartes from Lanchara ruled for 28,800 years. After the death of Otiartus, his son Xisuthrus ruled for 64,800 years. The great flood occurred during his reign. In total, this makes 10 monarchs who ruled for 432,000 years. The information can be summarized as follows:

1.   Alorus – 36,000 years

2.   Alaparus – 10,800 years

3.   Almelon – 46,800 years

4.   Ammenon – 43,200 years

5.   Amegalarus – 64,800 years

6.   Daonus – 36,000 years

7.   Edovanchus – 64,800 years

8.   Amempsinus – 36,000 years

9.   Otiartes – 28,800 years

10.   Xisuthrus – 64,800 years

This totals 10 kings who ruled for a combined 432,000 years.

These are the figures related in Alexander Polyhistor's book. If one considers this to be accurate history and accepts the validity of reigns lasting for such vast spans of years, then that person would also need to believe other incredible material found in the same book. Nonetheless, I will relay what Berosus says in the same historical narrative and will continue the account that Alexander Polyhistor has included in his book. One after another, he recounts these types of things.

In the first of his Babylonian books, Berosus claims that he lived during the time of Philip's son, Alexander, and that he wrote based on numerous books that were carefully kept in Babylon, covering a period of 215 myriad years, including chronologies, historical accounts, the Creator's making of Heaven, Earth, and the Seas, and information about kings and their deeds...

In the first year, within the boundaries of Babylonia, an awesome creature named Oannes emerged from the Red Sea. According to Apollodorus, this being had the complete body of a fish. However, by the fish's head was another human head, and by the tail were a pair of human feet. It could speak human language. A likeness of Oannes has been preserved to this day. The creature would spend the day among humans, abstaining from any food, and would instruct people in letters, the techniques of various arts, including city and temple building, knowledge of laws, the nature of weights and measures, and how to collect seeds and fruits. In fact, he taught humankind everything necessary for domestic life on earth. Since then, no one has discovered more. At sunset, the Oannes creature would return to the sea, remaining in the vast waters until morning, living as an amphibian. Later, other similar creatures emerged, as the book of the kings makes clear. Furthermore, it is said that Oannes wrote about deeds and virtues, giving humankind words and wisdom.

[5] There was a time, he says, when all was dark and water covered everything. Various sorts of creatures existed on earth. Some could reproduce themselves asexually, while others could procreate and give birth to humans with two wings, others with four wings and two faces, one

body and two heads, both male and female, and others having both male and female natures combined. Some humans had the legs of goats, horns on their heads, and others had the hooves of horses. Some had the rear half of a horse and the front half of a human. Others had a hybrid appearance, part horse and part bull. Also born were bulls with human heads, dogs with bodies having the flippers of a fish and a fish's tail sprouting from the hindquarters. There were horses with dogs' heads and humans and other creatures with horses' heads or human forms and the extremities of fish. Additionally, there were various dragon-shaped creatures, hybrid fish, reptiles, snakes, and many astonishing creatures of differing appearances. Images of each of them are preserved in the temple of Belus. All of them were ruled by a woman named Markaye, who was called T'aghatt'ay in Chaldean. The Greek translation of T'aladday is "sea." While these mixed creatures were emerging, Belus attacked. He split the woman (the sea) in two, making half into the sky and the other half into the earth, killing the creatures within it."

NOTE: It's worth noting that Berosus' account of hybrid species might suggest genetic engineering in the remote past and match up with the description of the thousand year old "alien mummies" shown to the Mexican congress in 2023 as shown here. If you search online, you'll find personal attacks, ridicule of the findings and other propaganda to suggest they are a hoax, *but not actual scientific rebuttals of the evidence*. For an actual evidence-based rebuttal, the only thing you will find is speculative skepticism or pretentious silence born out of hubris. The actual genetic analysis that was done showed they have DNA not similar to any known species on Earth and were said to have a mix of human and non-human DNA, with some sequences that did not match any known organism in the databases used for comparison. The carbon dating of the samples indicates an estimated age of over a thousand years. The presence of unique genetic material, combined with the morphological features of

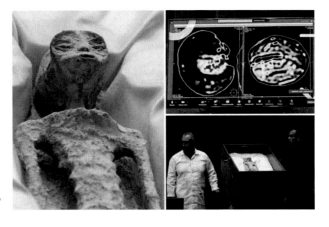

these mummies—such as their elongated skulls, three fingered hands and what appears to be eggs in one of their abdomens—has led some to speculate that they may represent evidence of a previously unknown species or even the result of genetic manipulation by an advanced civilization. One person even suggested they might not even be dead but dormant. Could a find such as this sync with Berosus' descriptions of ancient hybrid creatures? If so, it might suggest that our understanding of prehistory and the capabilities of ancient peoples is a lot more erroneous than we have been led to believe. Could discoveries such as these point to a lost (*or intentionally buried*) chapter in human history?

The myths of the Sumerians, it is believed, made their way to the Hurrians, the Hebrews, the Hittites, and through the latter, to the Ancient Greeks, though it is also just as likely they may have all shared the same proto source that was much more ancient. As time passed, so did the tales as they morphed and evolved along with the languages, leaving only a kernel of truth from what was originally told and which might have been, at one time, an oral history from a now forgotten history. With the Ancient Greeks, Hesiod provides a possible account of this lost age of man as follows:

> **"The gods and mortal humans share the same origins. In the very beginning, a Golden Generation of shining-faced humans was created by the immortals who dwell in the homes of Olympus. This was during the time of Kronos when he ruled the heavens.** These beings lived like gods, with spirits free from anxiety, labor, or sorrow. Old age did not burden them, and their bodies did not change. They enjoyed feasts, free from all evils, and when they died, it was like falling into a peaceful sleep. They had everything they needed, and the earth, without being prompted, provided them with an abundance of produce. They lived in peace, with wealth and flocks, and were beloved by the blessed gods.
>
> This Golden Generation became superhumans, known as *daimones*, existing by the will of Zeus. They are the guardians of justice and protectors against evil acts, roaming the earth enveloped in mist. They were given the privilege of bringing prosperity, a kingly honor.
>
> After the Golden Generation, the gods created a second, much worse generation—the Silver Generation. Unlike the Golden Generation, they were neither in nature nor in understanding. These people were raised by their mothers for a hundred years, playing ineptly at home. When they finally matured, they lived only briefly, suffering because they could not avoid hubris and neglected to honor the gods. Zeus, angry with them, hid them away because they did not give proper honor to the gods. When the earth covered this generation, they were called the blessed, though they too were mortals, living below the earth but still receiving a share of honor.
>
> Next, Zeus created a third generation, the Bronze Generation, born from ash trees. These beings were violent and terrible, obsessed with the deeds of war and acts of hubris. They did not eat grain, and their hearts were hard as rock. They had great strength and powerful limbs. Their tools, homes, and weapons were all made of bronze, and there was no black iron. They destroyed each other with their own hands and went nameless to the dark house of Hades, leaving behind the bright light of the Sun.
>
> When this Bronze Generation was also covered by the earth, Zeus created yet another generation, the fourth, which was just and better—the godlike generation of heroes, called demigods. They lived throughout the boundless earth and were overcome by war and battle. Some died at the walls of Thebes, others at Troy, fighting over Helen. Zeus granted them a special place to live at the edges of the earth, far from the immortal gods, with Kronos as their king. They dwell with

carefree hearts on the Islands of the Blessed, near the deep-swirling river Okeanos, where they enjoy a honey-sweet harvest three times a year.

Finally, comes the Fifth Generation, the Iron Generation, to which we belong. This is a time of toil and suffering, where good and bad are mixed. Even this generation will be destroyed when children are born with gray hair at their temples. Relationships will break down—between father and child, guest and host, and friend and friend. The just and the good will no longer be honored, while the wicked and the arrogant will be. Envy and violence will dominate, and Aidōs and Nemesis will leave the earth, leaving behind only misery for humankind."

The belief in prior ages of humanity was not unique to the Ancient Greeks; other civilizations held similar views. The Ancient Egyptians, for example, recorded a deep prehistory in texts like Manetho's writings and the Turin King List, which trace the lineage of rulers far back into Egypt's mythical past. Additionally, both Herodotus and Diodorus Siculus mentioned seeing a series of statues representing ancient Egyptian priests, suggesting a priesthood lineage that extended well beyond 10,000 BCE.

Turin King List:

The Turin King List, also known as the Turin Royal Canon, is a hieratic papyrus dating to the reign of Ramesses II (circa 13th century BCE). It lists the names of kings of Egypt from the earliest times until the New Kingdom, though parts of it are fragmentary and some rulers' names are missing or illegible. Before the historical rulers, the list mentions as Egypt's rulers:

1. **Ra** (the sun god)
2. **Shu** (god of air)
3. **Geb** (god of the earth)
4. **Osiris** (god of the afterlife)
5. **Set** (god of chaos and violence)
6. **Horus** (god of kingship and the sky)
7. **Thoth** (god of wisdom and writing)
8. **Demigods and Spirits: Shemsu-Hor** (Followers of Horus): Semi-divine beings believed to have ruled Egypt after the gods and before the pharaohs. They are often associated with the legendary period when Egypt was unified.

Manetho's Account:

Manetho was an Egyptian priest from Sebennytos who lived in the 3rd century BCE. His work, *Aegyptiaca*, written in Greek, provides a history of Egypt, including lists of rulers from both the divine and human realms. Manetho's list begins with gods and demigods, much like the Turin King List.

1. **Ptah**: Often identified with Hephaestus by the Greeks, Ptah was believed to be the creator god in Memphis.
2. **Ra**: The sun god, equivalent to Helios.
3. **Shu**: God of the air.
4. **Geb**: God of the earth.
5. **Osiris**: God of the underworld.
6. **Isis**: Goddess of magic and motherhood.
7. **Horus**: God of kingship and the sky.
8. **Set**: God of chaos and the desert.
9. **Thoth**: God of wisdom and writing.
10. **Ma'at**: Goddess of truth and justice.
11. **Heliopolitan Spirits**: Also referred to as the "Spirits of the Dead," these were thought to have ruled for a significant time after the gods and before the first human kings.
12. **Shemsu-Hor** (Followers of Horus): These were the demigods or divine beings that ruled Egypt after the gods and before the first human kings. They are said to have ruled for thousands of years.

Modern scholarship would have us believe the above were imaginary creations; with no reality, but another alternative presents itself, that these were human beings that ruled and were deified, and remembered thousands of years after they died, and based on the writings of the Ancient Egyptians, the above were likely not even native to Egypt, but from a place known as Punt and Aaru, the latter which was known as the Egyptian Underworld. Do any writings from Ancient Egypt from these God-kings survive?

The *Corpus Hermeticum* is a collection of texts that were highly regarded during the Renaissance as works of profound antiquity, believed to contain the wisdom of ancient Egyptian priests and pharaohs. These writings were attributed to Hermes Trismegistus, a legendary figure thought to be a synthesis of the Greek god Hermes and the Egyptian god Thoth, who was on the list above as one of the mythical rulers of Ancient Egypt. The *Corpus Hermeticum* was translated into Latin in the 15th century by the scholar Marsilio Ficino at the behest of Cosimo de' Medici, who believed these texts held the key to ancient and divine knowledge, and Ficino even put his translations of Plato on hold to work on the *Corpus Hermeticum*. As time went on, propaganda from certain religious authorities and scholars suggested that these works were not from Ancient Egypt but were instead the invention of writers in the 2nd century CE, during the early Roman Empire. However, more recent analysis has found that, while the texts were indeed compiled during that period, the source material is rooted in much older Egyptian antiquity. This suggests that the *Corpus Hermeticum* preserves and transmits the ancient wisdom of the pharaohs as it was claimed, and which presents a quite different picture than the backward beliefs the Egyptians are traditionally depicted as having. These works suggest a blend of influences from distant lands such as India and Tibet, emphasizing the importance of meditative focus, the avoidance of unattainable desires to prevent suffering, and the cultivation of moral character. They also convey the belief that upon death that the mind is reborn in a new body.

The influence of the *Corpus Hermeticum* was far-reaching, shaping the thoughts and works of many key figures of the Renaissance. It inspired thinkers like Giovanni Pico della Mirandola, who saw in these texts a synthesis of all religious and philosophical traditions, as well as figures such as Giordano Bruno, who used Hermetic ideas to challenge the dogmas of the Church, and was burned alive at the stake for doing so. Even Sir Isaac Newton, known for his groundbreaking work in physics, was influenced by Hermetic thought, incorporating it into his studies of alchemy and the natural world. The following passage is taken from the Corpus Hermeticum and contains an ancient dialogue, *The Secret Sermon on the Mountain*, between Hermes Trismegistus and his son Tat and is likely similar to the stories the Pharaohs of Ancient Egypt would have been taught and known:

> **1.** "Father," Tat began, his voice filled with curiosity, "you spoke to me earlier in riddles about the divine. You mentioned that no one could be saved without experiencing something you called 'Rebirth,' but you never explained what that meant. When I sought your guidance, especially during our journey up the mountain, you told me that I would only learn about Rebirth when I became a stranger to the world. So, I prepared myself, distancing my mind from the distractions of this world. Now, please, fulfill your promise and teach me about Rebirth. I don't understand where or how a person is born again, or from what seed this new life comes."

> Hermes, with a knowing smile, responded, "Rebirth comes from wisdom, a deep understanding that arises in silence. The seed from which this new life grows is True Goodness."

> Tat, still puzzled, asked, "But who sows this seed, Father? I feel lost."

> "The seed is sown by the Will of the Divine," Hermes explained.

> "And what is the nature of the one who is born from this, Father?" Tat pressed on. "Is this new being a child of the Divine?"

> "He is the Atum in all things, composed of all powers," Hermes replied, his tone calm and assuring.

> Tat furrowed his brow, "You speak in riddles, Father. You're not explaining this to me plainly."

> Hermes sighed, "This divine knowledge, my son, cannot be taught. It is something that, when the time is right, the Divine helps you remember."

> **3.** Tat, growing frustrated, pleaded, "Father, you're telling me things that seem impossible. I need direct answers. Am I not your true son? Explain to me the nature of this Rebirth."

> "What can I say, my son?" Hermes responded thoughtfully. "Whenever I look within myself and find clarity through the mercy of the Divine, I realize that I have passed through my old self and emerged

into a new, eternal form. I am no longer the person I once was; I have been reborn in mind. This path to Rebirth isn't something that can be taught, nor can it be seen with the physical eyes with which you see the world."

4. "Father," Tat said, his voice tinged with desperation, "you've thrown me into a whirlwind of thoughts and confusion. I can't even see myself clearly anymore."

Hermes gazed at him gently, "I wish, my son, that you could move beyond your current self, like those who dream while still awake."

"Please, Father," Tat urged, "tell me, who is responsible for this Rebirth?"

"It is the Son of the Divine, the Atum who embodies all, born from the Will of the Divine," Hermes explained.

5. Tat, now deeply bewildered, murmured, "Father, I don't understand. My senses are failing me... I see your greatness, but it seems so far beyond my comprehension."

Hermes smiled gently, "Even in this, you misunderstand, my son. The physical form you see is not the true self; it changes with each passing day. It grows and diminishes because it is not a permanent thing."

6. "What then is true, Father?" Tat asked earnestly.

"True is that which is never disturbed, which has no shape, no color, no form. It is the light within, something that cannot be changed or contained by anything physical," Hermes replied, his voice calm and steady.

Tat felt his mind spinning. "I'm losing my grip on reason, Father. Just when I thought I was gaining wisdom, I find myself more confused than ever."

Hermes nodded, understanding his son's turmoil. "This is how it is, my son. The world you know is made up of things you can see and touch, but the true essence of life cannot be perceived in this way. It's like trying to grasp air with your hands—you feel something, but you can't hold onto it."

7. "Am I not capable of understanding this, Father?" Tat asked.

Hermes shook his head, "No, my son. It's not that you're incapable. It's just that you need to turn inward, to search within yourself. When you do, you'll find the answers you seek. Quiet your physical senses, and your inner divinity will awaken. Cleanse yourself of the things that tie you to the material world."

Tat looked at his father, wide-eyed. "Do I really have such things within me, Father?"

"Yes," Hermes replied, "many, and they are fierce."

Tat frowned, "I don't understand them, Father."

"Your first obstacle is ignorance, my son," Hermes explained. "Then come grief, intemperance, lust, unrighteousness, greed, error, envy, deceit, anger, recklessness, and malice. These are the things that bind you to the physical world. But, with the mercy of the Divine, these obstacles can be overcome, one by one. This is the journey of Rebirth."

8. Hermes then instructed, "Now, my son, be still and remain silent. This silence allows the mercy of the Divine to continue flowing to you. Rejoice, for you are being purified, preparing yourself to receive the truth. When you gain true knowledge of the Divine, ignorance will be cast out. And when joy fills you, sorrow will flee."

9. "Now, I call upon the strength of self-control to push away desire," Hermes continued. "See how righteousness takes its place when unrighteousness is gone? As we rid ourselves of these burdens, we make room for the good, for truth, and for light. As these virtues fill us, the darkness cannot remain."

10. "You see now, my son, the path of Rebirth," Hermes said with a gentle smile. "When the powers of good replace the burdens of the past, true understanding is born. In this Rebirth, we become like gods, filled with light and life, and with this, we find true happiness."

11. Tat, his eyes wide with awe, exclaimed, "Father, I feel it! I see beyond with a new clarity. I am not just here—I am everywhere! In the heavens, on earth, in the water, in the air—I am part of it all!"

Hermes nodded, "Yes, my son, this is Rebirth. You are no longer bound by the limitations of the physical body. This is the true freedom of the spirit."

12. "But tell me, Father," Tat asked eagerly, "how do the powers of good drive out the obstacles of darkness?"

Hermes explained, "The body, my son, is made of twelve elements, each representing different aspects of life. They seem separate, but they are actually one. When the ten powers of good come into play, they naturally push out the twelve obstacles of darkness. The ten powers give birth to the soul, uniting life and light into one."

13. Tat, filled with wonder, said, "Father, I see it all now. I see myself clearly in this new light."

"This, my son, is the true Rebirth," Hermes said. "It's not about seeing the world with your eyes, but with your inner mind, beyond the physical."

14. Tat then asked, "Father, will this body, made up of these powers, ever be destroyed?"

Hermes gently hushed him, "Do not speak of things that cannot be. The physical body will change and eventually die, but the true essence within, the one you have now discovered, will never perish. Do you not realize, my son, that you have been born a god, just as I have?"

15. Tat, filled with reverence, said, "Father, I long to hear the hymn of praise you heard when you reached the higher realm."

Hermes smiled, "Just as I was told by the Shepherd, my son, when I reached the higher realm, the Eight. You are ready now, for you have been made pure."

16. "Father, please, let me hear it," Tat pleaded.

"Be still, my son," Hermes said softly. "Listen to the hymn of Rebirth—a hymn so sacred that it is kept in silence. Stand where the sky is open, facing the southern wind as the sun sets, and give thanks. Then, do the same at sunrise, facing the east wind. Now, be still."

The Sacred Hymn

17. "Let all of creation hear my hymn! Open, Earth! Let the Abyss be unlocked for me. Be still, Trees! I am about to sing praises to the Creator, the Atum who is All. Heavens, open, and Winds, be still! Let the eternal Sphere of the Divine hear my words! For I will praise Atum, the One who made everything, who set the Earth in place, who hung the heavens, who commanded the ocean to give life-giving water to the land, for all to use. He made the Fire shine for gods and men alike, for every purpose. Let us all together give praise to Atum, the ruler above the heavens, the Lord of all creation! He is the Eye of the Mind; may He accept the praise of my inner powers!"

18. "Powers within me, sing praises to Atum, the One and All! Sing with my will, all powers within me! O blessed knowledge, you have illuminated me; through you, I sing praises to the Light that only the mind can see. I rejoice in the joy of the Mind. Sing with me, all you powers! Sing praises, my self-control; sing through me, my righteousness, the praises of the righteous; sing, my sharing-with-all, the praises of the All; through me, sing, Truth, the praises of Truth! Sing, O goodness, the good! O Life and Light, our praises flow to you! Father, I give you thanks; You, the energy of all my powers; I give You thanks, O Divine One, You, the power of all my energies!"

19. "Your Word sings through me Your praises. Take back through me all that is Yours—my offering of reason! Thus cry the powers within me. They sing Your praise, O All; they do Your Will. From You comes the Will; to You returns the All. Receive from all their reasonable offerings. O Life, preserve all that is within us; O Light, illuminate it; O Divine One, inspire it. It is Your Mind that guides Your Word, O Creator, Bestower of Spirit upon all."

20. "For You are the Divine Atum, and Your creation calls out to You through fire, through air, through earth, through water, and through spirit, through all living things. From Your eternal realm, I have found praise-giving; in Your Will, the object of my search, I have found peace."

Tat, filled with awe, said, "Father, by your grace, I have seen this praise-giving. I have set it within my own inner world too."

Hermes smiled, "Yes, my son, place it within the world that only your mind can see."

Tat nodded, "Yes, Father, in that world I have placed it; for your hymn and praise-giving have illuminated my mind. Now, I too wish to offer my own praise-giving to the Divine Atum."

21. "Do so thoughtfully, my son," Hermes advised.

Tat, with deep reverence, said, "I offer my words of praise to you, O Father of my being, as one offers to the Divine. O Divine Atum and Father, You are the Lord, You are the Mind. Receive from me offerings as You will, for by Your Will all things have been perfected."

Hermes, with a nod, said, "Send your offering, son, acceptable to the Divine Father of all; but remember to add, 'through the Word.'"

Tat, with gratitude, replied, "Thank you, Father, for teaching me to sing such hymns."

22. Hermes, with a warm smile, concluded, "I am happy, my son, that you have brought forth the good fruits of Truth, products that cannot die. Now that you have learned this lesson from me, promise to keep your virtue hidden and do not reveal the way of Rebirth to others. We have both given this sufficient attention, both I, the speaker, and you, the listener. Through the Mind, you have come to know yourself and our common Father."

The Shipwrecked Sailor from the Middle Kingdom, dating back to around 2200 BCE, is an ancient Egyptian text that tells the tale of a sailor who survives a shipwreck and encounters a mystical serpent on a remote island. In this tale, the serpent refers to itself as the "Lord of Punt" and speaks of a star that fell from the sky and destroyed his island and his relatives:

> "A wise servant once said, "Take heart, my lord. We have arrived home at last. The ship is anchored, the ropes are secured, and the bow has touched the shore. Thanks have been given to the gods, and everyone has embraced each other in relief. Our sailors have returned safely, with none lost, even after our journey to the farthest reaches of Nubia. We are home again, and in peace. Listen to me, my lord, though I am but a humble man. Refresh yourself, wash your hands, and prepare your mind to speak with the King. Remember, a man's words can save him or bring him shame, so speak from your heart and answer without hesitation."

> The shipwrecked traveler then began to recount his tale:

> "I will tell you of my own experience, of what happened to me when I was on a journey to the king's copper mines. I set out to sea in a ship that was 225 feet long and 60 feet wide, with a

crew of 150 of Egypt's best sailors. These were men who knew the sky and the land, whose hearts were wiser than lions. They could predict storms before they came and knew when a squall was about to rise. Yet, despite their skills, a storm overtook us at sea. Before we could reach land, the wind intensified, and a massive wave, 12 feet high, crashed over us. A plank of wood was hurled toward me, and I grabbed it. As for the ship, everyone on board perished; I was the only one who survived.

A wave carried me to an island, where I spent three days alone, with only my own thoughts for company. I found shelter in a thicket and wandered the island in search of food. There, I discovered figs, grapes, and all kinds of large berries. There were gourds, melons, and enormous pumpkins, as well as fish and waterfowl. The island provided everything I needed. After I had eaten, I left the rest of the food on the ground, for I could carry no more. I dug a hole, lit a fire, and offered a sacrifice to the gods.

Suddenly, I heard a sound like thunder, which I thought was the sea. The trees shook, and the ground trembled. I covered my face and saw a serpent approaching. It was 45 feet long, with a beard over three feet in length, and its body was covered in golden scales. The ridges above its eyes were pure lapis lazuli, shimmering blue. The serpent coiled itself before me and opened its mouth. I lay flat on my stomach before it, and it spoke to me:

'Who brought you here? Who brought you here, you miserable creature? If you don't tell me who brought you to this island, I will make you vanish like smoke.'

I was too stunned to reply. The serpent then took me in its mouth and carried me to its resting place, where it set me down unharmed. Again, it asked, 'Who brought you to this island in the sea, surrounded by waves?'

I answered, with my hands humbly folded before it, 'I was on a mission from the king, traveling to the mines in a ship with 150 of Egypt's best sailors. But a storm arose, splitting our ship in two. I alone was saved, and a wave brought me to this island.'

The serpent, seemingly appeased, said to me, 'Do not fear, little one. It is by the grace of God that you have been spared and brought to this island, where there is no shortage of food. You will remain here for four months, after which a ship will arrive to take you back to your homeland, where you will live out your days.'

The serpent continued, 'Let me tell you my own story. I once lived here with 75 of my brethren and children, and with a young girl who was dear to me. But one night, a star fell from the sky, and they all perished in flames. Only I survived, and now I am alone. But you, if you are strong, will return to your family and your home.'

I bowed deeply before the serpent and said, 'I will tell the king of your power and greatness. I will bring you offerings of incense and perfumes, the finest treasures of Egypt. I will make sure that you are honored in my city, and sacrifices will be made to you as befits a god loved by those in faraway lands.'

The serpent laughed and said, 'You speak of incense, but you have little of it in Egypt. I am the prince of Punt, where the finest myrrh is found. Once you leave this place, you will never see this island again, for it will vanish into the waves.'

As predicted, a ship arrived, and I recognized those aboard. I told the serpent, but it already knew. The serpent said, 'Farewell, little one. Return to your home, see your children, and make sure my name is honored in your city.'

The serpent gave me gifts: myrrh, incense, spices, ivory, and other treasures. I loaded these into the ship, thanked the serpent, and sailed away. Two months later, I returned to Egypt and presented the king with the gifts. The king praised me before his nobles and appointed me to his personal guard.

So now, my lord, look upon me as I stand here, having returned to my homeland after all I have seen and experienced. Listen to my words, for it is wise to heed the counsel of others."

The prince replied, "Do not make yourself out to be perfect, my friend. Does one give water to a goose in the morning when it is to be slaughtered by day's end?"

And so ends the Tale of the Shipwrecked Sailor, as recorded by the skilled scribe Ameni-Amen-aa. May life, strength, and health be his!"

NOTE: The "Lake Iliamna Monster" is said to inhabit Lake Iliamna, the largest lake in Alaska. Descriptions of Illie vary, but it is reported to be around 30 feet long, with some accounts suggesting it could be even longer. The creature is typically described as having a long, serpentine body, and video and photographic evidence suggests it is similar to other reported lake monsters like the Loch Ness Monster. It is often believed that these are dinosaurs or some other unknown sea creature by those that take the reports seriously, but what is never  suggested, is that the reason they haven't been discovered is that perhaps they represent intelligent life, especially given one eyewitness account of the Lake Iliamna Monster where the head was described as gigantic, and where they observed him and his wife on a boat, which could indicate a very large brain. If so, then it could suggest *The Shipwrecked Sailor* might be the first historical record of interactions with other non-human intelligent species that live on our planet, or perhaps elsewhere in our solar system such as the oceans of Europa, but choose not to interact with us now for the same reason Grebennikov indicated in his book when he describes how aliens might flee from our planet when they see how we treat, torture, slaughter and devour other life as if only we have any importance, or the right to exist.

Moving on to other legends the *"Book of the Heavenly Cow"* is an Ancient Egyptian text that details Ra's wrath against humanity, leading to the near-destruction of mankind. The story centers on Ra's decision to send his Eye, in the form of the goddess Hathor, to annihilate the rebellious humans:

> "This story takes us back to a time when the gods of Egypt walked among men, fully understanding their desires and needs. At this time, Ra, the Sun-god, ruled as king over Egypt. However, Ra was not the first in the line of divine rulers. Before him, Hephaistos, as mentioned by the historian Manetho, reigned for 9,000 years, while Ra's reign lasted only 992 years according to some sources, or less than 100 years according to others.

> Regardless of the exact length of his reign, it seems that Ra, who was known as the "self-created and self-begotten" god, had ruled over humanity for a very long time. His subjects began to murmur against him, complaining that he was old, with bones like silver, a body like gold, and hair as blue as lapis lazuli. Hearing these complaints, Ra summoned his bodyguard and ordered them to bring all the gods who had been with him in the primeval World-ocean to the Great House, a temple that could only be the famous sanctuary at Heliopolis.

> When Ra entered the Great Temple, the gods paid homage to him and took their places on either side. Ra informed them of the complaints of the humans he had created with his Eye. He asked for their advice, as he was reluctant to punish the rebels without first hearing what the other gods had to say. The gods advised Ra to send forth his Eye to destroy the blasphemers, for no one on earth could resist its power, especially when it took the form of the goddess Hathor. Ra followed their counsel, sending Hathor in her terrifying form to hunt down and annihilate the rebels, who had fled to the mountains in fear. Hathor was relentless in her pursuit and slaughtered them without mercy. She reveled in her bloody work, and when she returned, Ra praised her for her actions.

> The bloodshed began at Suten-henen (Herakleopolis), and during the night, Hathor waded through the blood of men. Ra asserted his dominance over the rebels, a moment referenced in the Book of the Dead, Chapter XVII, where it is said that Ra first rose as king in Suten-henen. Osiris was also crowned in this city, where the legendary Bennu bird, or Phoenix, was said to dwell, alongside the "Crusher of Bones".

> Ra ordered messengers to bring him large quantities of a fruit called "tataat" from the city of Elephantine. The fruit was given to Sekti, a goddess of Heliopolis, to crush and grind, after which it was mixed with human blood and added to a large brewing of beer made by female slaves. They produced 7,000 vessels of this mixture. Ra approved of the brew and had it sent up the river to

where Hathor was still engaged in her slaughter. During the night, the beer was poured out into the meadows of the Four Heavens. When Hathor arrived, she drank deeply of the beer, which contained human blood and mandrakes, and became so intoxicated that she paid no further attention to the humans.

Pleased, Ra welcomed Hathor, calling her "Amit," meaning "beautiful one," and from that time on, "beautiful women" were said to be found in the city of Amit, located in the Western Delta near Lake Mareotis. Ra decreed that at every festival held in his honor, "sleep-producing beer" should be brewed, and the number of vessels should match the number of Ra's handmaidens. These festivals, which started as religious observances, eventually degenerated into drunken and licentious orgies under the influence of these "beautiful women," who were believed to resemble Hathor.

Following this, Ra expressed his weariness with humanity, complaining that his limbs were weak for the first time in his life. Ra was pleased with the repentance of those who had turned back to him, and he forgave them for their righteous slaughter of his enemies. Ra then announced to Nut that he intended to leave the earth and ascend into heaven. He declared that all who wished to see him must follow him there. Upon ascending, he created the "Field of Peace" (Sekhet-hetep) and the "Field of Reeds" (Sekhet Aaru), which became the Elysian Fields of the Egyptians, a paradise for the blessed dead. He also created the stars, which the legend likens to flowers, and fearing that Nut might collapse under the weight of the heavens, he caused the Four Pillars of Heaven to come into being. Ra entrusted Shu with the task of supporting the heavens, making him the new Sun-god in his place.

As the story progresses, Ra, remembering that he had once been bitten by a serpent and nearly lost his life, decided to eliminate the threat of serpents to his successors. He summoned Keb, the Earth-god, and instructed him to wage war against all the serpents in his domain. Ra also promised to impart the secret word of power he had used to protect himself to magicians and snake-charmers, as well as to his son Osiris, ensuring that they would be immune to serpent bites. This decree laid the foundation for the ancient profession of snake-charmers, who were believed to have received their knowledge directly from Ra.

Finally, Ra summoned Thoth and took him to the Tuat, the Other World, where he gave him authority over all who dwelled there. Thoth was to act as Ra's vicar, punishing the wicked and ensuring that Ra's light continued to shine in the Tuat. Ra's abdication was complete, and he entrusted Thoth with the power to rule in his place, ensuring that the wicked were kept at a distance and that Ra's legacy would endure even after he left the earth."

Sanchuniathon, a Phoenician historian that is believed to have lived around 1,200 BCE, claimed that his work was grounded in ancient, secret texts of the Ammoneans, which he uncovered from inscriptions within Phoenician temples. According to his account, these writings revealed a truth that had been obscured over time: the gods worshiped by the ancients were once human beings, later deified after their deaths. Sanchuniathon suggested that the Phoenicians took the names of their rulers and assigned them to cosmic elements, leading to the veneration of natural forces like the sun, moon, and stars. This approach reflects a form of euhemerism, where mythological tales are interpreted as veiled histories of real people and events. His interpretation offers a radical departure from the allegorical and mythological traditions, proposing that what were once mortal kings were later immortalized as gods by their followers. In Eusebius' *Praeparatio Evangelica*, he writes:

Philo, having divided the entire work of Sanchuniathon into nine books, introduces the first book with this preface about Sanchuniathon:

"These things being so, Sanchuniathon, a man of great learning and curiosity, eager to uncover the earliest history of all nations from the creation of the world, diligently sought out the history of Taautus. He knew that Taautus was the first to invent letters and begin the writing of records. Thus, he based his history on Taautus, whom the Egyptians called Thoyth and the Alexandrians called Thoth, translated by the Greeks into Hermes."

Following this, Philo criticizes more recent authors for distorting the legends of the gods into allegories and theories, saying:

"But the most recent writers on religion dismissed the real events from the beginning, instead inventing allegories and myths and forming fictitious connections to cosmic phenomena. They established mysteries and covered them with absurdities, making it difficult to discern what truly happened. Sanchuniathon, however, discovered secret writings of the Ammoneans, which were hidden in shrines and not known to everyone. He diligently studied them, discarded the original myths and allegories, and completed his work. Later priests attempted to hide this again and restore the mythical character, which led to the rise of mysticism, something that hadn't previously influenced the Greeks."

Philo continues:

"I discovered these things in my pursuit of understanding Phoenician history and through thorough investigation, not relying on Greek accounts, which are contradictory and written more to provoke debate than to seek truth."

And later, Philo adds:

"My conviction that these facts are as Sanchuniathon described them grew after seeing the disagreements among the Greeks. As a result, I composed three books titled 'Paradoxical History.'"

Philo further explains:

"It's important to clarify that the most ancient peoples, particularly the Phoenicians and Egyptians, who passed down their traditions to the rest of humanity, considered those who discovered the necessities of life or contributed significantly to society to be the greatest gods. They honored these benefactors as gods after their deaths, building shrines, consecrating pillars, and naming staves after them. The Phoenicians revered these figures and celebrated them during their greatest festivals, often naming elements of the cosmos after their kings and those regarded as gods. However, their concept of gods was limited to natural forces such as the sun, moon, stars, and elements, with some gods being mortal and others immortal."

Philo, after laying out these points in his preface, begins interpreting Sanchuniathon's work, starting with the theology of the Phoenicians:

"The first principle of the universe was air, dark with cloud and wind, or rather a blast of cloudy air, and a turbid chaos as dark as Erebus. These were boundless and without limit for many ages. But when the wind became enamored with its own origins and mixed with them, this connection was called Desire. This was the beginning of all creation, though the wind itself had no knowledge of its own creation. From this union, Mot was produced, which some say is mud, and others describe as a decayed watery compound. From this came every germ of creation and the generation of the universe. Certain animals without sensation emerged from it, and from them grew intelligent beings called 'Zophasemin,' meaning 'observers of heaven,' formed in the shape of an egg. Mot also brought forth light, the sun, moon, stars, and the great constellations."

This is their cosmogony, which introduces clear atheism. Let's now examine how he describes the generation of animals:

"When the air burst into light, both the sea and the land became heated, generating winds, clouds, and heavy downpours. After the elements were separated and displaced by the sun's heat, they collided in the air, producing thunder and lightning. The intelligent animals, previously described, woke up startled by the sound and began moving on land and sea, both male and female."

This is their theory of the generation of animals. Next, the writer adds:

"These things were found written in the cosmogony of Taautus and his Commentaries, derived from his conjectures and evidence that his intellect discerned, discovered, and made clear to us."

He continues by mentioning the names of the winds Notos, Boreas, and others:

"They were the first to consecrate the earth's produce, regarding them as gods and worshipping them as essential to life for themselves and future generations. They offered drink offerings and libations."

He further notes:

"These were their concepts of worship, reflecting their weakness and timidity. He then says that from the wind Colpias and his wife Baau (which he translates as 'Night') were born Aeon and Protogonus, mortal men. Aeon discovered food from trees. Their offspring, Genos and Genea, inhabited Phoenicia. During droughts, they stretched their hands to heaven towards the sun, whom they regarded as the lord of heaven, calling him Beelsamen, which in Phoenician means 'lord of heaven,' or 'Zeus' in Greek."

After this, Philo criticizes the Greeks:

"It is not without reason that we have explained these things in many ways, to address the later misinterpretations of the names in the history, which the Greeks, in their ignorance, misunderstood due to the ambiguity of translations."

He continues:

"From Genos, son of Aeon and Protogonus, were born mortal children named Light, Fire, and Flame. They discovered fire by rubbing pieces of wood together and taught its use. They had sons of great size and stature, who gave their names to the mountains they inhabited, such as Mount Cassius, Libanus, Antilibanus, and Brathy. From them were born Memrumus and Hypsuranius, who got their names from their mothers, as women in those days had free relationships with any man they met."

Philo then states:

"Hypsuranius lived in Tyre and built huts out of reeds, rushes, and papyrus. He quarreled with his brother Ousous, who invented clothing from the skins of wild beasts. When violent rains and winds occurred, trees in Tyre rubbed together and caught fire, burning down the woods. Ousous took a tree, stripped it of branches, and was the first to venture out on the sea. He consecrated two pillars to fire and wind, worshipped them, and offered blood from the wild beasts he hunted."

"But when Hypsuranius and Ousous died, their survivors consecrated staves to them, worshipped their pillars, and celebrated festivals in their honor. Many years later, from the descendants of Hypsuranius, were born Agreus and Halieus, the inventors of hunting and fishing. From them came two brothers who discovered iron and how to work it. One of them,

Chrysor, practiced oratory, incantations, and divinations and was identified as Hephaestus. He invented the hook, bait, line, and raft, and was the first to make a voyage. Therefore, he was revered as a god after his death and was also called Zeus Meilichios. Some say his brothers invented brick walls. Later, two youths were born from their lineage, one named Technites (Artificer) and the other Geinos Autochthon (Earth-born Aboriginal). They devised the mixing of straw with clay to make bricks and drying them in the sun, and they also invented roofs. From them, others were born, including Agros and Agrueros or Agrotes, who added courtyards, enclosures, and caves to houses. From them came farmers and hunters, also known as Aletae and Titans. From these were born Amynos and Magus, who established villages and sheepfolds. From them came Misor and Suduc, meaning 'Straight' and 'Just.' They discovered the use of salt."

"Misor was the father of Taautus, who invented the first written alphabet. The Egyptians called him Thoyth, the Alexandrians Thoth, and the Greeks Hermes. Suduc was the ancestor of the Dioscuri, Cabeiri, Corybantes, or Samothraces, who are said to have invented the ship. From them came others who discovered herbs, the healing of venomous bites, and charms. During their time, a certain Elioun, called 'the Most High,' and a female named Beruth were born, and they lived near Byblos."

"From them was born Epigeius or Autochthon, later called Uranus, from whom the element above us was named because of its beauty. His sister, Ge, was named after the Earth. Their father, the Most High, died in a battle with wild beasts and was deified, and his children offered libations and sacrifices to him."

"Uranus, having succeeded his father's rule, married his sister Ge, and they had four sons: Elus (also called Kronos), Baetylus, Dagon (also known as Siton), and Atlas. Uranus also fathered many children with other wives, which angered Ge and led to their separation."

"After leaving Ge, Uranus would return to her with violence whenever he pleased and tried to destroy their children. However, Ge repelled him many times with the help of allies. When Kronos reached adulthood, he, with the counsel and help of Hermes Trismegistus (his secretary), repelled Uranus and avenged his mother."

"Kronos had two children, Persephone and Athena. Persephone died a virgin, but with the advice of Athena and Hermes, Kronos made a sickle and an iron spear. Hermes used magical words to inspire Kronos's allies to fight against Uranus on behalf of Ge. Kronos engaged in war, drove Uranus from power, and took the throne. In the battle, Kronos captured Uranus's beloved concubine, who was pregnant. Kronos gave her in marriage to Dagon, and in his house, she gave birth to Uranus's child, Demarus."

"After this, Kronos built a wall around his dwelling and founded the first city, Byblos in Phoenicia."

"Soon after, Kronos became suspicious of his brother Atlas and, with Hermes's advice, threw him into a deep pit and buried him. Around this time, the descendants of the Dioscuri built rafts and ships and made voyages. They consecrated a temple near Mount Cassius, and the allies of Elus, who is Kronos, were called Eloim, and those who followed Kronos were known as Kronii."

"Kronos, having a son named Sadidus, killed him with his own sword out of suspicion, becoming a murderer of his son. Similarly, he beheaded one of his daughters, causing all the gods to fear Kronos's nature."

"But as time passed, Uranus, in exile, secretly sent his maiden daughter Astarte and her sisters Ehea and Dione to kill Kronos by deception. However, Kronos captured them and, though they were his sisters, made them his wives. When Uranus learned of this, he sent Eimarmene and Hora with other allies to attack Kronos, but Kronos won them over to his side."

"Furthermore, Uranus devised the Baetylia, bringing stones to life. Astarte bore seven daughters to Kronos, known as the Titanides or Artemides. Rhea bore seven sons, the youngest of whom was deified at birth. Dione bore daughters, and Astarte again bore two sons, Desire and Love. Dagon, after discovering corn and the plow, was called Zeus Arotrios."

"One of the Titanides married Suduc, who was called 'the Just,' and gave birth to Asclepius."

"In Peraea, Kronos fathered three sons, Kronos (of the same name as his father), Zeus Belus, and Apollo. During their time, Pontus, Typhon, and Nereus, father of Pontus and son of Belus, were born."

"From Pontus came Sidon, who, with her sweet voice, invented musical song, and Poseidon. Demarus fathered Melcathrus, also known as Hercules."

"Uranus then waged war against Pontus, and after revolting, allied himself with Demarus, who attacked Pontus. However, Pontus defeated Demarus, who vowed an offering if he escaped."

"In the thirty-second year of his reign, Elus (Kronos) ambushed Uranus in an inland location, captured him, and emasculated him near some fountains and rivers. Uranus was deified there, and as he died, his blood spilled into the waters. The site is still pointed out today."

This is the story of Kronos, and these are the tales of the golden age of the Greeks, whom they describe as the first and 'golden race of articulate-speaking men,' reflecting the blissful happiness of the past.

The historian then adds:

"Astarte, the greatest goddess, Zeus Demarus, and Adodus, king of the gods, reigned over the land with Kronos's consent. Astarte placed a bull's head on her own as a symbol of royalty, and during her travels around the world, she found a fallen star, which she consecrated on the holy island of Tyre. The Phoenicians say that Astarte is the same as Aphrodite."

"Kronos, while traveling the world, gave the kingdom of Attica to his daughter Athena. During a plague, Kronos offered his only son as a whole burnt offering to his father Uranus and circumcised himself, forcing his allies to do the same. Later, another son of his by Rhea, named Muth, died, and Kronos deified him. The Phoenicians call him Thanatos and Pluto. After this, Kronos gave the city of Byblos to the goddess Baaltis, also known as Dione, and Berytus to Poseidon, the Cabeiri, the Agrotae, and the Halieis, who also consecrated the remains of Pontus at Berytus."

"Before this, the god Taautus imitated the features of the gods who were his companions—Kronos, Dagon, and the others—and created the sacred characters of the letters. He also devised for Kronos the insignia of royalty: four eyes in front and behind, two of which were quietly closed, and four wings on his shoulders—two spread for flying and two folded."

"The symbol meant that Kronos could see when asleep and sleep while awake; similarly, the wings indicated that he could fly while at rest and rest while flying. The other gods had two wings on their shoulders, signifying that they accompanied Kronos in his flight. Kronos himself had two wings on his head, representing the all-ruling mind and sensation."

"When Kronos traveled to the South, he gave all of Egypt to the god Taautus as his royal dwelling place. These things were first recorded by Suduc's seven sons, the Cabeiri, and their eighth brother, Asclepius, as the god Taautus commanded them."

"Thabion, the first hierophant of the Phoenicians, allegorized all these stories and mixed them with physical and cosmic phenomena. He delivered them to the prophets who celebrated the orgies and inaugurated the mysteries. These prophets, seeking to increase their influence, handed these stories down to their successors and foreign visitors. One of these visitors was Eisirius, the inventor of the three letters and brother of Chna, the first to be called Phoenix."

Philo then remarks:

"The Greeks, with their superior intellect, appropriated most of these early stories and adorned them with the ornaments of tragic phrase and various embellishments to charm with their pleasant fables. Thus, Hesiod and the Cyclic poets created their theogonies, battles of giants, battles of Titans, and castrations. With these fables, they traveled and spread their myths, conquering and replacing the truth."

"Our ears, having grown accustomed to these fictions over the ages, now guard them as a trust. The mythology has become so ingrained that the truth is dismissed as nonsense, and the fabricated narrative is accepted as reality."

These are the words of Sanchuniathon, translated by Philo of Byblos, and affirmed as true by the philosopher Porphyry.

The Gaelic myths of the Tuatha Dé Danann offer another hint of a potentially lost prehistory. These legendary figures were said to have come to Ireland from four northern cities, echoing the myth of Hyperborea or even Atlantis, bringing with them advanced knowledge and medical abilities with descriptions that include what appears to be a silver robotic arm, and synthetic flesh being re-grown over it. In the myths, the Tuatha Dé Danann arrived in Ireland by way of flying ships that were then burned. The tales of their eventual defeat, and their retreat into the Otherworld, often described as an underground world, led to their association with "mound dwellers" or "hill folk" in modern times and ancient monuments like Newgrange and the Sidhe mounds.

In the ancient mythology of China, the concept of immortals, known as *Xian*, plays a central role in the stories of the distant past. These beings are described as having achieved eternal life through mastery of esoteric knowledge and spiritual practices. The Taoist texts are filled with accounts of such immortals who withdrew from the mundane world to live in the mountains, where they practiced alchemy, meditated, and perfected their spiritual energy or *qi*. The legend of the Jade Emperor starts with his origins as the crown prince of the kingdom of Pure Felicity and Majestic Heavenly Lights and Ornaments. From birth, he was marked by a light that filled the kingdom, a sign of his future role. As a young prince, he was known for his kindness and wisdom, helping those in need. After his father's death, he became king and ensured peace throughout his land. He then devoted himself to cultivating the Tao for 1,750 eons, attaining Golden Immortality, and eventually becoming the Jade Emperor after another hundred million years of cultivation.

A significant myth describes how the Jade Emperor became the ruler of all deities. In the early days, monstrous beings and demons roamed the earth, defying the immortals. The Jade Emperor, then an ordinary immortal, retreated to a mountain cave to cultivate the Tao, enduring 3,200 trials. Meanwhile, a malevolent entity amassed power and led an assault on heaven. After completing his cultivation, the Jade Emperor intervened in the battle, defeating the entity with his wisdom and benevolence, leading to his proclamation as the supreme sovereign of all gods, immortals, and humans.

The story of the Cowherd and the Weaver Girl, with its magical robe that enables Zhinü to descend from the sky to the earth, hints at elements of flight and advanced technology embedded in Chinese mythology. This concept of flight and the crossing of realms is not isolated. Other myths and legends also feature deities and immortals with the ability to traverse vast distances and even soar through the heavens. The story of *Chang'e*, the Moon Goddess, also involves an element of flight. After consuming an elixir of immortality, Chang'e ascended to the moon, where she resides to this day.

The ancient Chinese believed that immortals lived on mythical islands to the east, such as Mount Penglai. Emperor Qin Shi Huang sent an expedition led by Xu Fu to find the elixir of life on Mount Penglai, but the expedition never returned; some believe they were shipwrecked in Japan. He then sought immortality by consuming a mixture of mercury and powdered jade prepared by his alchemists. This so-called elixir of immortality ultimately caused his death. His tomb is reputed to contain rivers of flowing mercury, symbolizing the rivers of China, and the importance they placed on the element of mercury.

In ancient China and Tibet, mercury was believed to have life-extending properties, the ability to heal fractures, and general health benefits. Similarly, Khumarawayh ibn Ahmad ibn Tulun, a ruler of Egypt known for his extravagance, reportedly constructed a basin filled with mercury on which he would lie atop air-filled cushions to be gently rocked to sleep.

In Mexico, large quantities of mercury were discovered in 2014 in a chamber beneath the 1,800-year-old Temple of the Feathered Serpent in Teotihuacan, alongside jade statues, jaguar remains, and other artifacts, further indicating the historical significance and mystique surrounding mercury in various ancient cultures.

Chapter 31 of the *Samarangana Sutradhara*, an 11th-century treatise on architecture, delves into the operation of flying machinery. The author says he has witnessed many of the devices he describes. Among these are two wooden aircraft, or "vimanas": one "light" and shaped like a massive bird, and another "heavy" and temple-shaped. Both are described as containing a fire chamber that heats a container of mercury, enabling the aircraft to lift off the ground. However, the full details of their construction are intentionally omitted for ethical reasons:

> "The construction of the machines has not been explained
> For the sake of secrecy, and not due to lack of knowledge.
> In that respect, that should be known as the reason—
> They are not fruitful when disclosed."

India's ancient texts, particularly the Vedas and the great epics, the *Mahabharata* and the *Ramayana*, offer glimpses into a time that has been lost to history. The Vedas, among the oldest religious texts in the world, contain hymns that speak of cosmic events, battles between gods, and advanced knowledge that suggests a civilization of great antiquity.

In the *Rigveda*, the gods are described as waging war against the Asuras, a race of powerful beings. The battles between these two groups are not just physical but involve the use of what appears to be advanced technology, including flying chariots like the ones referenced above (*Vimanas*) and weapons of immense power, akin to modern nuclear devices. One hymn speaks of the god Indra wielding the *Vajra*, a thunderbolt weapon that could destroy entire cities. "Armed with the Vajra, Indra, the Thunderer, smote the cities of the Dasas..."

The *Mahabharata*, particularly in the *Bhagavad Gita* section, delves into the philosophy and duty of kingship but also contains descriptions of a devastating war that brought an end to an era. The war, known as the Kurukshetra War, is depicted as involving gods, demigods, and heroes who wielded divine weapons. The text also refers to the concept of Yugas, or ages, through which the world cycles, each one declining in virtue and length. The current age, the Kali Yuga, is seen as the final and most degenerate age, following a time of greatness and wisdom that has long passed.

A Middle Eastern folk tale in *One Thousand and One Nights* also references a "magic carpet" that is purchased in India, allowing one to be transported elsewhere: "Whoever sitteth on this carpet and willeth in thought to be taken up and set down upon other site will, in the twinkling of an eye, be borne thither, be that place nearhand or distant many a day's journey and difficult to reach."

Solomon's carpet, also known as the "Flying Carpet of Solomon," is a legendary artifact in Middle Eastern folklore. It was said to be a massive carpet large enough to carry Solomon's entire army, which he could command to transport them to any location with just a thought. This carpet, imbued with magical properties, could travel vast distances in mere moments, defying the limitations of time and space. In addition to the legendary flying carpet, the Ark of the Covenant is another artifact with mysterious power. Ancient writings describe that during the Battle of Jericho, the Israelites carried the Ark around the city walls for seven days. On the seventh day, after the priests blew their trumpets, the walls of Jericho collapsed. Uzzah, a man who touched the Ark to steady it, was struck dead on the spot suggesting electrocution. When the Israelites crossed the Jordan River, the priests carrying the Ark stepped into the river, and the waters parted, allowing them reportedly to cross on dry ground. The instructions for building the Ark of the Covenant are detailed in the Book of Exodus:

"They shall make an ark of *shittah* wood. Two cubits and a half shall be its length, a cubit and a half its breadth, and a cubit and a half its height. You shall overlay it with pure gold, inside and outside shall you overlay it, and you shall make on it a molding of gold around it. You shall cast four rings of gold for it and put them on its four feet, two rings on the one side of it, and two rings on the other side of it. You shall make poles of *shittah* wood and overlay them with gold. And you shall put the poles into the rings on the sides of the ark to carry the ark by them. The poles shall remain in the rings of the ark; they shall not be taken from it. And you shall put into the ark the testimony that I shall give you. "You shall make a mercy seat of pure gold. Two cubits and a half shall be its length, and a cubit and a half its breadth. And you shall make two cherubim of gold; of hammered work shall you make them, on the two ends of the mercy seat. Make one cherub on the one end, and one cherub on the other end. Of one piece with the mercy seat shall you make the cherubim on its two ends. The cherubim shall spread out their wings above, overshadowing the mercy seat with their wings, their faces one to another; toward the mercy seat shall the faces of the cherubim be. And you shall put the mercy seat on the top of the ark, and in the ark you shall put the testimony that I shall give you. There I will meet with you, and from above the mercy seat, from between the two cherubim that are on the ark of the testimony, I will speak with you...."

The Ark was simply a wooden chest overlaid with gold, with a cover called the mercy seat flanked by two gold cherubim. It was designed to be portable, with poles inserted through rings for carrying. In another ancient text, two vessels made of orichalchum were said to be situated by it in Solomon's Temple. One has to wonder if the *shittah* wood described here is similar to the wood used in the platform by Grebennikov as he described in Part Two of this book; a type of wood infected with the burrowed remains of a certain beetle's chitin, and whether this object resembles the object in the artwork of the Ancient Egyptians for their journey to Aaru. Much of the Hebrew legend for the Ark, for example, was likely inspired by a chest or a solar barque the Ancient Egyptians used in their rituals, or at least, believed their gods used.

For those who wish to build their own ark and experiment: constructing a simple wooden chest, like those seen in museum exhibits and depicted in the image to the left, *simply won't do*. You will need to

utilize a special type of wood, one infected with the remains of a specific insect species, and likely, a unique copper, silver and gold alloy, and probably along with the right materials to place within it. Other things such as unique frequencies might then be required to activate it, perhaps a ritual chant or a musical instrument similar to ones the Ancient Egyptians utilized? There are some clues from historical sources which might suggest what type of wood to look into. For example, the *Was scepter* used by pharaohs, what types of trees were used in their construction? If *acacia wood*, then certain trees infected by a specific flying beetle species might want to be considered. That might provide some general hints, and it is likely the biblical descriptions of *Aaron's Rod*, if there is any truth to it, originated from the capabilities of the *Was scepters,* which might have utilized organic technology that has been overlooked by researchers. Some Ancient Egyptian artifacts are said to consist of a wood *Diospyros ebenum* from Sri Lanka or Southern India, which some scholars believe might suggest a link between those areas and the land the Egyptians believed their gods came from: Punt. *Cedar, Sycamore fig* and *Juniper* could also be considered. The scepters themselves also utilized certain metals such as gold, electrum (*an alloy of gold and silver*), bronze and copper in their designs as well as precious stones.

As for the stones depicted inside the chest, if not for ceremonial or ritual use, then it is possible they might be materials with unique properties as well, perhaps similar to Plato's description of orichalchum.

If so, the usage of Carnelian stones in Ancient Egypt and elsewhere might reflect a memory of specific metallic alloys or other materials that exhibited quantum effects that involved time dilation. One possible clue comes to us from the Innishkea Islands of Ireland, which are believed by some to be a place where remnants of Druidism might have survived until as recently as two centuries ago. In the early 19th century, the islanders were discovered worshiping a stone they believed had the power to accelerate potato growth, calm the wind, and prevent fires. This *"godstone,"* as it was known, was eventually shattered by a pirate who, unable to set fire to a house where the stone was kept, vented his frustration on it. The remnants were later thrown into Portavally Harbor by a priest in 1890. The stone, reportedly weighing three pounds, was green in color and wrapped in red flannel. While this description probably suggests a mineral like malachite or a copper alloy with a green patina, if there is any truth to the legends, a modern and open-minded scientific perspective might want to investigate if that stone was a unique metamaterial exhibiting quantum effects. If so, taking a dive into the waters of Portavally Harbor and looking for a green stone that has been smashed into pieces could provide a clue to the alloy's composition (*assuming it is still there*).

If one has access to a substance that can manipulate time and gravity; it's worth noting that proper precautions would need to be taken for anyone entering into, or around, a field of time dilation. Light would shift into a different electromagnetic spectrum as the photons pass through the field. This goes for both light and sound coming from the outside in, which would shift to a lower spectrum, and anything within the field, would shift to a higher spectrum as it passes out. Visible light from the outside world could shift to the infrared, possibly requiring anyone within the field to wear goggles allowing them to see in the infrared range, otherwise they might find themselves in a darkened environment or where ultraviolet radiation shifts down to visible light. The world outside the field would likely appear as a still photo, or a slow motion video, and color could conceivably be affected as well if one was able to still see in the visible spectrum. The amplification would correspond to the amount of time dilation, but as a general rule, if time was dilated so that one second of our time becomes hours of experienced time for anyone within the bubble of time dilation, then light within the field might shift into ultraviolet, x-rays or even gamma ray radiation outside of it, and sound might shift to ultrasound, or be heard as a hum. This could make it very dangerous for anyone nearby, and likely, why the Ark of the Covenant, if it was a vehicle for time manipulation, would have been kept in the dark, and covered when it was moved. For those within the field, if one crossed the barrier while it was active, it would also result in part of their body being in normal time, and another part in dilated time, likely causing instant death due to a lack of blood flow or inability for the organs to function if blood flow was restricted. Therefore, one would need to be within the field before it is activated, and stay within it, until the device was deactivated. Entering it from the outside world while active, if that would even be possible, would likely be fatal. Sunscreen and protection from radiation should be used for those outside the field. Lead-lined garments might be necessary if gamma rays or x-rays are a concern. Eye protection, such as goggles designed to block out harmful wavelengths, would also be critical for safety. Given the legends surrounding the Ark, where individuals who merely looked at or touched it dropped dead, and considering reports from World War

II experiments involving flesh melting and radiation burns, it would be prudent to conduct any related experiments in a darkened environment to minimize the risk of visible light transforming into lethal radiation. While these ill effects may also have been caused by chemical burns or intense heat, appropriate safety measures should be taken to protect against these hazards as well, especially if a mixture of substances involving mercury—believed to be involved in alchemical experiments with the fabled Philosopher's Stone—are used. It is quite possible that fields of time dilation, when applied to various metals such as mercury, might affect their phase transition states and superconductivity, and where they might give off blackbody radiation at room temperature. For instance, if time dilation affects the atomic or molecular interactions within a material, it could change the temperature at which a substance transitions between solid, liquid, or gas phases. If it also affects the quantum states of electrons within a material, it could hypothetically alter the conditions under which superconductivity occurs. This might involve shifting the critical temperature or changing the material's ability to exhibit superconductivity altogether, and where it could potentially cause a material to emit blackbody radiation at temperatures where it normally would not, perhaps even at room temperature. This is all speculative, but all things to consider for what might occur to anything within the chest if time dilation is involved.

For those within the field, infrared goggles might be needed to navigate an environment where visible light may have shifted out of the normal spectrum. If the time dilation field alters the electromagnetic environment, devices or clothing that shield against electromagnetic interference might also be advisable to prevent disruption of any personal electronic devices. Outside the field, protective barriers or enclosures made of magnetic shielding materials could be set up around the perimeter of the field to minimize the risk of magnetic field exposure. This would be particularly important if the magnetic fields generated by the time dilation device were strong enough to pose a health risk to those nearby. To protect against strong magnetic fields, individuals within and outside the field should consider using materials such as mu-metal or other specialized alloys. These materials are designed to redirect and absorb magnetic field lines, thereby reducing the field's impact on sensitive equipment or the human body. For those within the field, wearing garments or suits that incorporate these magnetic shielding materials could help protect against any harmful effects, and a specialized helmet with additional shielding and a visor, would be highly recommended. Experiments to determine if air pressure is affected should also be done before entering into such an environment, as a sudden increase or decrease in air pressure could be fatal; as well as determining whether supplemental oxygen would need to be brought with if the field was active for a long period of time.

For those on the outside, the moment such a time dilated field became active, the person within it would likely become invisible due to the differences in the passage of time, unless they immediately deactivated the field. The reason for the invisibility likely has to do with the fact that when something travels at the speed of light, such as a photon, it does not experience time as we do. If someone hypothetically traveled at the speed of light, for example, from our sun to Alpha Centauri, while over four years of time would pass for people on Earth, they would experience the trip instantaneously as if no time had passed. This is a tough concept to grasp, but essentially, it means light can pass through a bubble of time dilation, but other things not moving at such high speeds, might not be able to. As for why an object becomes invisible, or is seen as an orb of light, or even a saucer, it is likely due to the fact that whenever we see something, what we are seeing is reflected light, so any light entering into a sphere of time dilated space, once it reflects back, will have to pass through minutes, hours or even days of dilated time, and will possibly shift to another electromagnetic spectrum not visible to us such as ultraviolet light, x-rays or gamma radiation. Additionally, if this effect involves phenomena beyond current physics, it could be that the information within the sphere is no longer connected to the universe outside, except for things traveling at light speed, where the uncertainty principle in quantum systems might allow the device's occupant to see the outside world while remaining invisible to it.

Assuming they moved about; the device's occupant might need to take precautions not to get too close to other people and observational experiments would need to be performed to understand the physical interactions and dangers. For example, Grebennikov mentions quite a few. In addition to visual protection, those on the outside might also require sound-dampening devices or ear protection to mitigate the effects of altered auditory frequencies. It is quite possible that matter outside the area of time dilated space might change in such an environment, and where what is solid in our experience of time, becomes something more atmospheric or fluid in theirs, or where they can pass through objects as if nothing is there and which does not enter the field, allowing them to pass through physical obstacles. There would be telltale signs time dilation was at play though; unexplained mold growth on surfaces, drafts of cold air, weird smells, batteries draining and going dead, strange insect or animal behavior, and those outside the field may confuse it as the sound of insects, a trilling noise (as is often described with crop circle formations), a series of high pitched clicks, an unexplainable hum, or they may hear nothing at all.

For any lifeforms that decided to live in such a time-dilated environment, their eyes would likely evolve to be larger than ours and have hardened corneas that are black or red, allowing them to see in the infrared range. In another case, if a city was built with such a substance, it could conceivably float in the sky and be invisible to us, and if it moved along with the Earth's rotation so it was always in daylight, then such a structure would be bathed in perpetual ultraviolet radiation which might shift down to visible light, but where the light might be diffused and come across as a sunset glow. In such an environment, one would not need to evolve eyes to see in the infrared range, but if genetic engineering were at play, one might design bodies that obtain energy from the sun rather than from food with skin that acts like solar panels. In other cases, if a civilization used this substance to create cities and structures underground or inside mountains within the Earth itself, it is possible the only light available would be light generated within the time dilated environment, such as any blackbody radiation emitted by this substance, and where larger eyes and the ability to see in the infrared would likely be an evolutionary advantage. In such a case, they may not obtain energy from the sun but other sources, or where they are buried in a location unable to receive any solar energy and become dormant. It's worth noting such a scenario could explain the myths of the Ancient Greeks. For example, after their defeat by the Olympian gods in the Titanomachy, the Titans were said to have been imprisoned in Tartarus, a deep, gloomy part of the underworld far beneath the surface of the Earth.

In comparative mythology, the myths of the Ancient Greeks are often regarded as unreliable for tracing the origins of Proto-Indo-European beliefs, primarily due to influences from the Near East and the pre-existing populations in Greece, who were likely connected to the Early European Farmers that settled in the region earlier. Despite these external influences, scholars generally agree that certain core themes can be traced back to the Proto-Indo-European religion.

One of the central beliefs across these cultures was in an Otherworld, often depicted as a realm like Hades, which one would reach by crossing a river or marsh. This realm was typically guarded by a creature, such as a dog, reflecting a widespread motif among Indo-European myths. Another recurring theme is the story of a divine figure battling a serpent or dragon, often using thunder as a weapon, and releasing the world's waters after defeating the creature.

Additionally, a creation myth involving twin brothers, Manu and Yemo, is believed to be of Proto-Indo-European origin. In this story, Manu kills Yemo, and from this act, mankind is created, with Yemo becoming the lord of the Underworld. This duality and the association of one brother with life and the other with death are common motifs in Indo-European myths. There are currently two main theories related to the origins of the Indo-Europeans, the Kurgan hypothesis, which believes that around 4,000 BCE, the

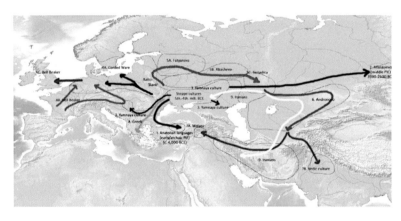

Indo-Europeans spread out from an area north of the Black Sea and made their way thousands of years later to places as far away as Britain and India, and which can be viewed to the left. However, a competing Anatolian hypothesis suggests that the Indo-European languages originated in Anatolia (modern-day Turkey) around 7,000 BCE or earlier, linking them to the Early European Farmers who lived there at the time. According to this theory, by around 6500 BCE, the Pre-Proto-Indo-European language in Anatolia began to diverge, leading to the development of the Anatolian languages and Archaic Proto-Indo-European. This Archaic Proto-Indo-European is then believed to have split further around 5000 BCE, giving rise to the Italic, Celtic, and Germanic language families in the Danube Valley, as well as Balkan Proto-Indo-European and the ancestor of the Tocharian languages. This theory is more in line with the genetic evidence, though the Kurgan hypothesis has more weight with academia currently due to the linguistic and archaeological evidence.

Regarding the Tocharian language family, some believe that some of the inhabitants of the Tarim Basin, where the Tarim mummies were found, might have spoken Tocharian around 2,000 BCE. A 2021 genomic study revealed that the earliest mummies from this region, dating from 2135 to 1623 BCE, had a significant amount of Ancient North Eurasian ancestry (about 72%) combined with a smaller percentage of Ancient Northeast Asian ancestry (about 28%), with no evidence of Western Steppe-related lineage. This suggests they were a genetically isolated group that adopted agricultural and pastoral practices from neighboring cultures, enabling them to sustain themselves along the oases of the Taklamakan Desert. While it was once believed that these individuals were "Proto-Tocharian-speaking pastoralists" and ancestors of the Tocharians, this theory has been largely discredited due to the lack of genetic ties with Indo-European-speaking groups.

Later mummies, however, from the Iron Age, particularly those from the Subeshi culture, exhibit features similar to the Saka (Scythian) Pazyryk culture of the Altai Mountains, especially in terms of weaponry, horse gear, and clothing. These Iron Age mummies are potential predecessors of the Tocharians. The more recent mummies from the Yanbulaq culture (1100-500 BCE), found in the easternmost parts of the Tarim Basin, present a mix of "Europoid" and "Mongoloid" characteristics, suggesting the area became a mixing pool due to migrations from East Asia.

Most of the Tarim mummies were discovered in the eastern end of the Tarim Basin, particularly around areas like Lopnur, Subeshi near Turpan, Loulan, and Kumul, as well as along the southern edge in places such as Khotan, Niya, and Cherchen (Qiemo).

Some of the most notable mummies include the tall, red-haired "Chärchän man" or "Ur-David" (1000 BCE), his son (also from 1000 BCE), and a one-year-old baby with brown hair, found with two stones positioned over its eyes. Another significant discovery is the "Hami Mummy" (c. 1400–800 BCE), a "red-headed beauty" unearthed in Qizilchoqa, as well as the "Witches of Subeshi" (4th BCE) discussed in Part One, who wore distinctive 2-foot-long black felt conical hats with flat brims. At Subeshi, a man with traces of a surgical operation on his abdomen was also found, with the incision sewn up using horsehair sutures.

It is believed the Taklamakan Desert's extreme dryness played a crucial role in the preservation of these mummies, however, the area was reportedly not as arid back then, which means perhaps that interpretation needs to be revisited? Many have been found in remarkably good condition, with intact hair ranging from blond to red to deep brown, often long, curly, and braided. Their clothing and textiles suggest a common origin with Indo-European Neolithic clothing techniques or a shared low-level textile technology. For example, Chärchän man wore a red twill tunic and tartan leggings, with the tartan-style cloth showing similarities to fragments from the Hallstatt culture in Austria. The preservation conditions also allowed for the identification of tattoos on mummies from several sites around the Tarim Basin, including Qäwrighul, Yanghai, Shengjindian, Shanpula (Sampul), Zaghunluq, and Qizilchoqa.

Textile analysis has shown that the fabrics found with the mummies are of an early European type, with close similarities to fragmentary textiles found in Austrian salt mines dating back to the second millennium BCE. Anthropologist Irene Good, an expert in early Eurasian textiles, noted that the woven diagonal twill pattern indicated the use of a sophisticated loom, making these textiles the easternmost known examples of such weaving techniques.

The cemetery at Yanbulaq contained 29 mummies dating from 1100 to 500 BCE. Of these, 21 were of Asian origin—the earliest Asian mummies found in the Tarim Basin—while eight belonged to the same Caucasian physical type as those found at Qäwrighul.

In 1995, Victor Mair asserted that the earliest mummies discovered in the Tarim Basin were exclusively of Caucasoid, or Europoid, origin. He posited that East Asian migrants only began arriving in the eastern portions of the Tarim Basin around 1,000 BCE, while the Uyghur peoples did not appear until approximately 842 CE. Mair's research team suggested that these early inhabitants may have arrived in the region via the Pamir Mountains around 5,000 years ago. Mair also claimed that these findings necessitate a reexamination of ancient Chinese texts that describe historical or legendary figures of great height, with deep-set blue or green eyes, long noses, full beards, and red or blond hair—features that were once dismissed but now seem potentially accurate.

In 2007, the Chinese government permitted a team to analyze the DNA of these mummies. The team

successfully extracted undegraded DNA from the mummies' tissues, revealing that the Tarim Basin was continuously inhabited from 2000 BCE to 300 BCE. Preliminary results indicated that the people of the Tarim Basin had diverse origins, including Europe, Mesopotamia, the Indus Valley, *and other regions yet to be determined*.

Between 2009 and 2015, 92 individuals from the Xiaohe Tomb complex were analyzed for Y-DNA and mtDNA markers. The analysis revealed that the maternal lineages of the Xiaohe people originated from both East Asia and West Eurasia, while the paternal lineages were exclusively West Eurasian. Notably, the East Eurasian mtDNA found in the Tarim mummies was similar to subclades found in southeast Siberians like the Udeghe and Evenks, rather than East Asians.

A significant discovery was that nearly all the males (11 out of 12) belonged to Y-DNA haplogroup R1a1-M17, now most common in Northern India and Eastern Europe. This finding suggests a strong genetic connection to these regions. A genetic study published in 2021 further supported this, showing that the Tarim mummies had a high level of Ancient North Eurasian ancestry, particularly from the Afontova Gora 3 population, with smaller contributions from Ancient Northeast Asians. This made the Tarim mummies one of the rare Holocene populations to derive most of their ancestry from Ancient North Eurasians.

Zhang et al. (2021) proposed that the "Western-like" features of the earlier Tarim mummies could be

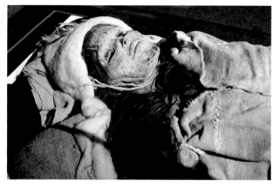

attributed to their Ancient North Eurasian ancestry, much as has been described to explain the same features in the Mandan Indians.

One of the most famous mummies is the "Princess of Xiaohe," uncovered in 2003 by archaeologists from the Xinjiang Institute of Archaeology. Dated to approximately 1800 BCE, she was found at the Xiaohe Cemetery, located 102 kilometers west of Loulan, at Nop Nur in Xinjiang. The Princess is particularly noted for her well-preserved appearance, including striking red hair and long eyelashes, which have captivated researchers and the public alike. She was dressed in a white wool cloak with tassels, a felt hat, a string skirt, and fur-lined leather boots, indicative of the clothing styles of her time. In her burial, the Princess of Xiaohe was accompanied by wooden pins and three small pouches filled with ephedra, a plant known for its stimulant and medicinal properties. Additionally, twigs and branches of ephedra were placed beside her body.

The Beauty of Loulan, also known as the "Beauty of Kroran," is another one of the most well-known Tarim mummies, discovered near Lop Nur in 1980. She lived around 1800 BCE and likely died at the age of 45 due to lung failure from inhaling sand, charcoal, and dust. It's believed here as well that the arid climate and preservative properties of salt kept her remains remarkably intact. She was buried in a woolen cloth. Her auburn hair was infested with lice, and she wore clothing made of wool and fur, including a felt hood with a feather, leather moccasins, and a woolen cap. Her

possessions included a comb, likely

used for both grooming and weaving, and a woven bag containing grains of wheat, indicating her preparation for the winter, a winter that likely killed her. Given that some were buried in coffins designed to look like boats and had stones covering their eyes, it is quite possible their burial practice provides a window into their beliefs and culture of an afterlife. Another thing worth considering is that, given that they were found in the Basin, perhaps they represented a group that had been exiled? If so, then perhaps an area nearby, such as the Kailash Mansarovar Region or the Tsangpo Gorge, could be worth exploring for the location of Hyperborea if these mummies have any connections at all to the Hyperboreans?

Although not stones, the Ancient Greeks practiced placing coins, known as obols, over the eyes or in the mouths of their dead. These coins served as payment for Charon, the mythological ferryman who transported souls across the River Styx to the underworld. The coins often featured images of Gorgons, mythical creatures said to inhabit a land at the edge of the known world. This motif bears a resemblance to the Epic of Gilgamesh, which may have inspired the Gorgon legend. Also in the epic, Gilgamesh embarks on a quest to find a plant at the bottom of the sea that grants immortality only to have it stolen by a serpent.

The idea of "exiles" is also found across the sea in Native America where the Navajo have a legend of Skinwalkers. It is believed by them that a Skinwalker is a former tribe member and a type of Navajo witch that has mastered both good and bad magic but is seduced by dark forces, and is recruited by a group where one of the rituals is they must engage in a form of cannibalism or sacrifice of one they love as an initiation ritual. Once initiated, they have the ability to shapeshift and take on the forms of other beings. This initiation idea may parallel the early mythic Indo-European myth of Manu, along with other well-known myths. In addition, early Christians might have been influenced by Near East and Graeco-Roman mystery religion practices that espoused a similar ritual to what is believed by the Navajo and their witches when they speak of eating the flesh and drinking the blood of Christ to obtain eternal life.

There are some writers that speculate the mythical figure of Moses was actually a Phoenecian named Moschus or Mochus of Sidon, who is believed to have lived around 1,300 BCE just after the conquest of Egypt of the Levant by Thutmose III. Strabo, Diogenes Laeterius, Posidonius and several others wrote that Mochus of Sidon was believed to have developed a theory of atomism and was the first one to propose that all matter is composed of small, indivisible particles—an early form of atomic theory. This would have been almost a thousand years earlier than Leucippus and Democritus in Ancient Greece, who are traditionally viewed as the founders of atomism. Very little is known about Mochus beyond brief mentions by those authors, who generally say he existed before the Trojan War. Incidentally, during the 18th Dynasty of Ancient Egypt, Akhenaten, a pharaoh known for his elongated skull similar to those found in Malta, ruled alongside his wife, Nefertiti, and their children. Akhenaten's reign (c. 1353–1336 BCE) was marked by a significant religious transformation in which he promoted the worship of the sun disk, Aten, as the primary deity, effectively introducing monotheism to Egypt. This period also saw the relocation of the capital to a new city, Amarna, built to honor Aten.

However, after Akhenaten's death, subsequent pharaohs, including Tutankhamun, reversed his religious reforms, restoring the traditional polytheistic beliefs. In an effort to erase his legacy, later rulers destroyed his monuments and attempted to remove Akhenaten's name from official records, as though he had never existed. The world's first conspiracy to remove those with elongated skulls from the official record, perhaps?

Another possibility suggesting a scientifically advanced civilization in ancient times is the potential connection between the builders of Stonehenge and the Ancient Egyptians. Author Andrei E. Zoblin claims that the layout of Stonehenge, when viewed from above, resembles Ancient Egyptian hieroglyphs that read "Eternally Living Atum" and encodes the atomic mass of hydrogen (1.0079). If this were somehow true, this would imply that whoever built Stonehenge had knowledge of Ancient Egyptian hieroglyphics and an understanding of atomic theory, specifically hydrogen.

Some have speculated that our modern word "atom," derived from the Ancient Greek "*atomos*," may have been influenced by the Egyptian word "Atum." Early atomism is traditionally attributed to the Greek philosophers Leucippus and Democritus as noted earlier—Leucippus and Democritus reportedly studied with Egyptian geometers, which might have influenced their usage of *atomos* which would mean the idea was of Egyptian, not Greek, origin. There are also those who believe Plato's concept of indivisible solids in the "Timaeus" represents a form of atomism, likely influenced by Pythagorean thought. Plato associated each Platonic solid with one of the classical elements: earth (cube), air (octahedron), water (icosahedron), and fire (tetrahedron), with the dodecahedron representing a fifth unknown element called the aether. This early form of atomism suggested that these solids were the building blocks of the physical world, much like modern quantum theory uses quarks to describe matter's fundamental constituents.

While Platonic solids bear little resemblance to modern quantum theory, there is a thematic parallel in the way both systems use geometry. In Loop Quantum Gravity (LQG) theory, space itself is quantized, implying discrete structures at the Planck scale. Just as molecules form crystalline structures, quantum geometry in LQG could be seen as a kind of cosmic crystallization at the fundamental level.

Some authors, such as myself, have wondered if Plato was referring to phase transitions and states of matter, with the classical elements representing gas, liquid, solid, plasma, and possibly a fifth state like Bose-Einstein condensates or gravitational force, and whether our understanding of three-dimensional space and linear time might limit our insight into these concepts at the quantum level, suggesting that the structure of the universe, and by extension, the states of matter, might be governed by quantized geometries beyond our current framework and conceptions.

Although speculative, if future advances in quantum theory were to reveal a connection between quantized geometries and the Platonic solids, it could suggest that Plato, Pythagoras, and others were in possession of a more advanced understanding of quantum theory than is currently acknowledged; one that perhaps the Ancient Egyptians pharaohs and priests had access to but did not share with the multitude as stated in the dialogue from the *Corpus Hermeticum,* and which trickled down to Mochus, Leucippus and Democritus.

Then, there is Plato's Atlantis, which I will not go over here but would direct the reader to my book *Atlantis & Its Fate In The Postdiluvian World*, which treats that subject in detail. If evidence were to emerge of an advanced antediluvian civilization, it is quite conceivable that their technology was based on principles derived from a deeper understanding of nature's intrinsic laws. While the above ideas do not prove that quantum theory existed in antiquity, they raise questions that could be explored through further research.

As for the Hyperboreans, if we consider a possible connection between Pythagoras and Abaris, exploring Pythagorean beliefs could offer insights into the culture and spirituality of the Hyperboreans. In addition, from the few sources we have concerning the Druids, it is also worth noting that Pythagoreanism and Druidism share many similarities. Both traditions believed in reincarnation, though they may have approached it in slightly different ways. Pythagoras and his followers were said to have believed that the soul transmigrates through different bodies over lifetimes, a belief documented in ancient sources like Diogenes Laërtius. Similarly, the Druids, as mentioned by Julius Caesar in his "Commentarii de Bello Gallico," believed in the transmigration of souls; as Caesar noted their warriors had no fear of death in battle.

Both the Pythagoreans and the Druids were seen as keepers of sacred knowledge. Pythagoras founded a brotherhood where initiates were trained in the secrets of their school, all of which were considered deeply spiritual and made inaccessible to the uninitiated. The Druids, too, held a similar role within Celtic society. They were the intellectual elite, responsible for maintaining and transmitting oral knowledge across generations. One had to study for decades with intense memorization skills to become a Druid. This knowledge was guarded closely, much like the Pythagorean secrets.

Our knowledge of the Druids is limited, relying heavily on a few historical mentions, many of which are believed to be second-hand accounts, likely derived from the now-lost works of Poseidonius. The most famous description of the Druids comes from Julius Caesar in *The Gallic Wars*. However, these accounts may reflect Roman biases rather than an accurate portrayal, often depicting the Druids as barbaric. In reality, they might not have been as savage as described. For instance, the notorious "Wicker Man" sacrifice, where a group of people—typically violent criminals—were allegedly burned alive inside a large wooden effigy, is reported by Caesar, but some scholars question whether such practices were ever conducted. More importantly, even if the Wicker Man ritual were true, it fundamentally bears a resemblance to modern executions by electric chair, where society, even today, essentially subjects violent criminals to being burned alive.

The Roman emperor Tiberius outlawed Druidism, and the few Druids who survived in Ireland and Britain were eventually persecuted and exterminated by Christians in the following centuries. While the Druids are commonly associated with the Celts, some theories suggest they may have had pre-Celtic origins and were later assimilated by Celtic invaders. The truth, however, remains elusive. What is more certain is that their philosophy closely resembled that of Pythagoras.

The ancient Roman geographer Pomponius Mela wrote that the Druids' teachings were secretive, conducted in forests and caves. Diodorus Siculus noted that they adhered to the Pythagorean doctrine, believing in the immortality of the soul and its transmigration into a new body after a set number of years. Whether these accounts are accurate or influenced by Poseidonius, who also wrote a now-lost commentary on Plato's *Timaeus* comparing it to Pythagoreanism, is unclear. However, one notable parallel between the Druids and the followers of Pythagoras is the inclusion of women, who were welcomed into their orders and treated as equals.

The earliest mention of the Druids comes from **Diogenes Laërtius**, who writes:

> "Some say that the study of philosophy originated with the barbarians. In that among the Persians there existed the Magi, and among the Babylonians or Assyrians the Chaldaei, among the Indians the Gymnosophists, and among the Celts and Gauls men who were called Druids and Semnothei, as Aristotle relates in his book on magic, and Sotion in the twenty-third book of his *Succession of Philosophers*. They say that the Gymnosophists of India and Druids instruct through riddles, urging the worship of the gods, abstinence from evil, and the practice of manly virtue."

It's worth noting that Aristotle's book *On Magic* and Sotion's *Succession of Philosophers* are lost, but they appear to have differentiated between various people and a revered group among them, possibly connecting the Druids to the same revered groups in Persia, Babylon, Syria and India.

Julius Caesar, who lived from 100 BC to 44 BC, provides one of the most detailed accounts of the Druids in his work *Commentarii de Bello Gallico* (The Gallic Wars), written around 58–50 BC. Caesar's observations, although often colored by his perspective as a Roman general, remain one of the primary sources on Druidic practices in Gaul. He writes of them as follows:

> "But of these two orders, one is that of the Druids, the other that of the knights. The former are engaged in things sacred, conduct the public and the private sacrifices, and interpret all matters of religion. To these a large number of the young men resort for the purpose of instruction, and

they [the Druids] are in great honor among them. For they determine respecting almost all controversies, public and private; and if any crime has been perpetrated, if murder has been committed, if there be any dispute about an inheritance, if any about boundaries, these same persons decide it; they decree rewards and punishments; if any one, either in a private or public capacity, has not submitted to their decision, they interdict him from the sacrifices. This among them is the most heavy punishment. Those who have been thus interdicted are esteemed in the number of the impious and the criminal: all shun them, and avoid their society and conversation, lest they receive some evil from their contact; nor is justice administered to them when seeking it, nor is any dignity bestowed on them. Over all these Druids one presides, who possesses supreme authority among them. Upon his death, if any individual among the rest is pre-eminent in dignity, he succeeds; but, if there are many equal, the election is made by the suffrages of the Druids; sometimes they even contend for the presidency with arms. These assemble at a fixed period of the year in a consecrated place in the territories of the Carnutes, which is reckoned the central region of the whole of Gaul. Hither all, who have disputes, assemble from every part, and submit to their decrees and determinations. This institution is supposed to have been devised in Britain, and to have been brought over from it into Gaul; and now those who desire to gain a more accurate knowledge of that system generally proceed thither for the purpose of studying it.

The Druids do not go to war, nor pay tribute together with the rest; they have an exemption from military service and a dispensation in all matters. Induced by such great advantages, many embrace this profession of their own accord, and [many] are sent to it by their parents and relations. They are said there to learn by heart a great number of verses; accordingly some remain in the course of training twenty years. Nor do they regard it lawful to commit these to writing, though in almost all other matters, in their public and private transactions, they use Greek characters. That practice they seem to me to have adopted for two reasons; because they neither desire their doctrines to be divulged among the mass of the people, nor those who learn, to devote themselves the less to the efforts of memory, relying on writing; since it generally occurs to most men, that, in their dependence on writing, they relax their diligence in learning thoroughly, and their employment of the memory. They wish to inculcate this as one of their leading tenets, that souls do not become extinct, but pass after death from one body to another, and they think that men by this tenet are in a great degree excited to valor, the fear of death being disregarded. They likewise discuss and impart to the youth many things respecting the stars and their motion, respecting the extent of the world and of our earth, respecting the nature of things, respecting the power and the majesty of the immortal gods.

The nation of all the Gauls is extremely devoted to superstitious rites; and on that account they who are troubled with unusually severe diseases, and they who are engaged in battles and dangers, either sacrifice men as victims, or vow that they will sacrifice them, and employ the Druids as the performers of those sacrifices; because they think that unless the life of a man be offered for the life of a man, the mind of the immortal gods can not be rendered propitious, and they have sacrifices of that kind ordained for national purposes. Others have figures of vast size, the limbs of which formed of osiers they fill with living men, which being set on fire, the men perish enveloped in the flames. They consider that the oblation of such as have been taken in theft, or in robbery, or any other offense, is more acceptable to the immortal gods; but when a supply of that class is wanting, they have recourse to the oblation of even the innocent.

They worship as their divinity, Mercury in particular, and have many images of him, and regard him as the inventor of all arts, they consider him the guide of their journeys and marches, and believe him to have great influence over the acquisition of gain and mercantile transactions. Next to him they worship Apollo, and Mars, and Jupiter, and Minerva; respecting these deities they have for the most part the same belief as other nations: that Apollo averts diseases, that Minerva imparts the invention of manufactures, that Jupiter possesses the sovereignty of the heavenly powers; that Mars presides over wars. To him, when they have determined to engage in battle, they commonly vow those things which they shall take in war. When they have conquered, they sacrifice whatever captured animals may have survived the conflict, and collect the other things into one place. In many states you may see piles of these things heaped up in their consecrated spots; nor does it often happen that any one, disregarding the sanctity of the case, dares either to secrete in his house things captured, or take away those deposited; and the most severe punishment, with torture, has been established for such a deed.

All the Gauls assert that they are descended from the god Dis, and say that this tradition has been handed down by the Druids. For that reason they compute the divisions of every season, not by the number of days, but of nights; they keep birthdays and the beginnings of months and years in such an order that the day follows the night. Among the other usages of their life, they differ in this from almost all other nations, that they do not permit their children to approach them openly until they are grown up so as to be able to bear the service of war; and they regard it as indecorous for a son of boyish age to stand in public in the presence of his father.

Their funerals, considering the state of civilization among the Gauls, are magnificent and costly; and they cast into the fire all things, including living creatures, which they suppose to have been dear to them when alive; and, a little before this period, slaves and dependents, who were ascertained to have been beloved by them, were, after the regular funeral rites were completed, burnt together with them."

Diodorus Siculus, a Greek historian who lived during the 1st century BC, provides a detailed account of the Gauls and their customs in his work *Bibliotheca historica* (Library of History), specifically in Book 5, sections 27–32. His descriptions offer valuable insights into the practices and beliefs of the ancient Celtic peoples. Diodorus Siculus writes:

"The Gauls are very tall with white skin and blond hair, not only blond by nature but more so by the artificial means they use to lighten their hair. They continually wash their hair in a lime solution, combing it back from the forehead to the back of the neck. This process makes them resemble Satyrs and Pans, as it makes the hair thick like a horse's mane. Some shave their beards while others allow a short growth, but nobles shave their cheeks and allow the moustache to grow until it covers the mouth. As a result, their moustaches become mixed with food while they eat, but serve as a sort of strainer when they drink. They do not sit in chairs when they dine but sit on the ground using the skins of wolves or dogs. While dining, they are served by adolescents, both male and female. Nearby are blazing hearths and cauldrons with spits of meat. They honor the brave warriors with the choicest portion, just as Homer says that the chieftains honored Ajax when he returned after defeating Hector in single combat. They also invite strangers to their feasts, inquiring of their identity and business only after the meal. During feasts, it is their custom to be provoked by idle comments into heated disputes, followed by challenges and single combat to the death. They do not fear death but subscribe to the doctrine of Pythagoras that the human spirit is immortal and will enter a new body after a fixed number of years. For this reason, some will cast letters to their relatives on funeral pyres, believing that the dead will be able to read them. In both journeys and battles, the Gauls use two-horse chariots that carry both the warrior and charioteer. When they encounter cavalry in battle, they first hurl their spears, then step down from the chariot to fight with swords. Some think so little of death that they fight wearing only a loincloth, without armor of any kind. They use free men from the poorer classes as charioteers and shield-bearers in battle. When two armies are drawn up for battle, it is their custom to step before the front line and challenge the best of their opponents to single combat, brandishing their weapons in front of them to intimidate the enemy. When an opponent accepts their challenge, they recite the brave deeds of both their ancestors and themselves, at the same time mocking the enemy and attempting to rob him of his fighting spirit. They decapitate their slain enemies and attach the heads to their horses' necks. The blood-soaked booty they hand over to their attendants, while they sing a song of victory. The choicest spoils they nail to the walls of their houses just like hunting trophies from wild beasts. They preserve the heads of their most distinguished enemies in cedar oil and store them carefully in chests. These they proudly display to visitors, saying that for this head, one of his ancestors, or his father, or he himself refused a large offer of money. It is said that some proud owners have not accepted for a head an equal weight in gold, a barbarous sort of magnanimity. For selling the proof of one's valor is ignoble, but to continue hostility against the dead is bestial. The Gauls wear stunning clothing—shirts dyed in various colors, and trousers they call bracae. They also wear striped cloaks with a checkered pattern, thick in winter and thin in summer, fastened with a clasp. They use uniquely decorated, man-high shields in battle, some with projecting bronze animals of superb workmanship. These animal-figures serve for defensive purposes as well as decoration. Their helmets have large figures on top—horns, which form a single piece with the helmet, or the heads of birds and four-footed animals—which give an appearance of added height to the warrior.

Their trumpets are also of a peculiar and barbaric kind, producing a harsh, reverberating sound suitable to the confusion of battle. Some use iron breastplates in battle, while others fight naked, trusting only in the protection which nature gives. They do not use short swords but prefer a longer variety hung on their right sides by chains of iron or bronze. Some wear gold or silver-plated belts around their tunics. Their spears, called lanciae, have iron heads a cubit [18 inches] or more in length and slightly less than two palms in width. Their swords are as long as the spears of other peoples, and their spears have heads longer than others' swords. Some of the spears have straight heads, but others are twisted along their entire length so that a blow not only cuts but mangles the flesh, and withdrawal tears the wound open. The Gauls are terrifying in appearance and speak with deep, harsh voices. They speak together in few words, using riddles that leave much of the true meaning to be understood by the listener. They frequently exaggerate their claims to raise their own status and diminish another's. They are boastful, violent, and melodramatic, but very intelligent and learn quickly. They have lyric poets called Bards, who, accompanied by instruments resembling lyres, sing both praise and satire. They have highly-honored philosophers and theologians [those who speak about the gods] called Druids. They also make use of seers, who are greatly respected. These seers, having great authority, use auguries and sacrifices to foresee the future. When seeking knowledge of great importance, they use a strange and unbelievable method: they choose a person for death and stab him or her in the chest above the diaphragm. By the convulsion of the victim's limbs and spurting of blood, they foretell the future, trusting in this ancient method. They do not sacrifice or ask favors from the gods without a Druid present, as they believe sacrifice should be made only by those supposedly skilled in divine communication. Not only during peacetime but also in war, the Gauls obey with great care these Druids and singing poets, both friend and enemy alike. Often when two armies have come together with swords drawn, these men have stepped between the battle lines and stopped the conflict, as if they held wild animals spellbound. Thus, even among the most brutal barbarians, angry passion yields to wisdom, and Ares stands in awe of the Muses. It is useful now to point out a distinction unknown to most. Those tribes that live inland from Massalia, as well as those around the Alps and on the eastern side of the Pyrenees, are called Celts. But those tribes in the northern area near the ocean, those near the Hercynian mountain [probably today in the Czech Republic], and those beyond as far as Scythia [present-day Ukraine and South Russia], are called Galatae. The Romans, however, group all these tribes together as Galatae. The women of the Gauls are not only as large as their husbands but are equal to them in strength. Gaulish children are usually born with gray hair, but this takes on the parents' color as time passes. The most savage tribes are those in the north and those which are near Scythia. Some say they eat human flesh, just like the Prettani [Britons] inhabiting the land called Iris [probably Ireland]. The savage and war-loving nature of the Gauls is well known. Some say that in ancient times they ravaged all of Asia under the name of Cimmerians, which in time became deformed to Cimbri. From long in the past it has been their nature to ravage foreign lands and view the rest of humanity as beneath them. It was they who captured Rome and plundered the temple at Delphi, and who extracted tribute from much of Europe and no small part of Asia. It was they who occupied the lands of the people whom they had defeated and were called Gallo-Graeci because of their connection with the Greeks, and who, last of all, destroyed many great Roman armies."

Dion Chrysostom, a Greek philosopher and historian who lived from around AD 40 to 120, offers insights into various cultures in his collection of speeches known as *Orations*. In *Oration* 49, specifically in section 24, he touches upon the Druids and their influence among the Celts. Dion Chrysostom writes:

> "The Persians have men known as Magi, the Egyptians have their holy men, and the Indians have their Brahmins. For their part, the Celts have men called Druids, who deal with prophecy and every division of wisdom. Even kings would not be so bold as to make a decision or take action without the Druids' counsel. Thus, in reality, it was the Druids who governed. The kings, who sat on golden thrones and lived luxuriously in their great residences, became mere agents of the decisions of the Druids."

Cicero, the renowned Roman statesman, orator, and philosopher who lived from 106 to 43 BC, discusses various forms of divination in his work *De Divinatione*. In Book 1, section 41.90, he specifically references the Druids and their practices among the Gauls. Cicero writes:

> "Nor is the practice of divination neglected even among the barbarian tribes, since indeed there are Druids in Gaul. Among these was Divitiacus the Aeduan, your guest and eulogist, whom I knew personally. He claimed a knowledge of the natural world which the Greeks call *physiologia*, making predictions of the future, sometimes by augury, sometimes by conjecture."

Ammianus Marcellinus, a Roman historian who lived from around AD 330 to 395, offers a detailed account of the late Roman Empire in his work *Res Gestae*. In Book 15, sections 9.4-8, he provides insights into the cultural and religious practices of the Gauls, including those of the Druids. Ammianus Marcellinus writes:

> "The Druids recount that part of the population of Gaul was indigenous, but that some of the people immigrated there from outlying islands and the lands beyond the Rhine, driven out by frequent wars and violent floods from the sea. Throughout these regions, as people gradually became more civilized, the study of praiseworthy doctrines grew, introduced by the Bards, Euhages [read Vates], and Druids. The Bards sang the praiseworthy deeds of famous men to the melodious strains of the lyre. The [Vates] endeavored to explain the sublime mysteries of nature. Between them were the Druids, an intimate fellowship of greater ability who followed the doctrine of Pythagoras. They rose above the rest by seeking the unseen, making little of human mortality as they believed in the immortality of the soul."

Pomponius Mela, a Roman geographer who lived between 37 and 50 CE, authored *De Situ Orbis* (The Description of the World), one of the earliest surviving works on geography. In Book 3, sections 2.18-19, he offers a glimpse into the practices of the Druids among the ancient Gauls. Pomponius Mela writes:

"The vestiges of savage customs still remain in the drawing of a victim's blood while he is being led to the altar, though outright slaughter has been abolished. Still, they have their own eloquence and wise men called Druids. They claim to know the size of the earth and cosmos, the movements of the heavens and stars, and the will of the gods. They teach, in caves or hidden groves, many things to the nobles in a course of instruction lasting up to twenty years. One of their doctrines has become commonly known to the populace so that warriors might fight more bravely: that the spirit is eternal and another life awaits the spirits of the dead. Thus they burn or bury articles useful in life with the dead. For this reason also, in past times, they would defer business and payment of debts to the next life. There were some who would even throw themselves willingly onto the funeral pyres of their relatives so that they might live with them still."

Pomponius Mela also describes a group of nine Druids on an island:

"Sena, in the Britannic Sea, opposite the coast of the Osismi, is famous for its oracle of a Gaulish god, whose priestesses, living in the holiness of perpetual virginity, are said to be nine in number. They call them Gallizenae, and they believe them to be endowed with extraordinary gifts to rouse the sea and the wind by their incantations, to turn themselves into whatsoever animal form they may choose, to cure diseases which among others are incurable, to know what is to come and to foretell it. They are, however, devoted to the service of voyagers only who have set out on no other errand than to consult them."

Pliny the Elder, a Roman author and naturalist who lived from 23/4 to 79 CE, composed *Natural History*, an extensive encyclopedia covering a wide range of topics, including the natural world and human practices. In Book 16, section 24, he discusses the Druids and their reverence for the mistletoe. Pliny the Elder writes:

"Not to be overlooked is the admiration of the Gauls for this plant [the mistletoe]. The Druids—as their magicians are called—hold nothing more sacred than this plant and the tree on which it grows, as if it grew only on oaks. They choose only groves of oak and perform no rites unless a branch of that tree is present. Thus it seems that Druids are so called from the Greek name of the oak [Greek drus]. Truly they believe that anything which grows on the tree is sent from heaven and is a sign that the tree was chosen by the god himself. However, mistletoe rarely grows on oaks, but is sought with reverence and cut only on the sixth day of the moon, as it is then that the moon is powerful but not yet halfway in its course (it is by the moon they measure days, years, and their cycle of thirty years). In their language, the mistletoe is called 'the healer of all.' When preparations for a sacrifice and feast beneath the trees have been made, they lead forward two white bulls with horns bound for the first time. A priest in white clothing climbs the tree and cuts the mistletoe with a golden sickle, and it is caught in a white cloak. They then sacrifice the bulls while praying that the god will grant the gift of prosperity to those to whom he has given it. They believe that mistletoe, when taken in a drink, will restore fertility to barren animals and is a remedy for all poisons. Such is the dedication to trifling affairs displayed by many peoples.

"Similar to the Sabine plant [Savin] is selagos. It is gathered without iron implements by passing the right hand through the left sleeve-opening of the tunic, as if one were stealing it. The harvester must be barefoot, dressed in white, and must have offered bread and wine before the gathering. The Gaulish Druids claim that selagos is a charm against every evil and that its smoke is a good remedy for eye diseases. They also gather a plant from marshes called samolus, which must be gathered with the left hand while fasting. This plant is used to treat diseases of cattle, but the gatherer must not look back during the process nor place the plant anywhere except in the drinking-trough.

There is also a sort of egg, famous in the [Roman] provinces of Gaul, but unknown to the Greeks. Innumerable snakes coil themselves into a ball in the summertime, secreting a substance that holds them together. This object is known as an 'anguinum.' The Druids say that as the snakes hiss, they cast the egg upwards, and it must be caught in a cloak before it touches the ground. One must immediately ride off on a horse with it, for the snakes will continue to pursue until the course of a stream blocks their way. If one tests it, the anguinum will float against the current of a river even when covered in gold. And, as the magi ['wizards'] often cloak their trickery in deception, they claim that these eggs must be taken only at a particular point in the lunar cycle, as if human beings could control the snakes' role in this process. Nonetheless, I have seen one of these eggs myself. It was round, the size of a small apple. The shell was cartilaginous, and mottled with cups like the tentacles of a squid. The Druids value it highly; it is praised as ensuring success in litigation and in securing audiences with kings. However, this is nonsense. For once, a man—a Roman knight and a tribesman of the Vocontii—held one of these eggs against his body during a trial and was condemned to death by the Emperor Claudius, seemingly for that reason alone.

The [Roman provinces of] Gaul also possessed magic down to the time of our memory. During the reign of Emperor Tiberius, a decree was issued by the Senate against the entire class of Druids, Vates, and physicians among the Gauls. Why do I mention this craft that has spread beyond the ocean to the far reaches of the earth? Nowadays, Britain continues to be held spellbound by magic and conducts so many rituals that it would seem Britain had given magic to the Persians. Peoples across the world are alike in this way, though they are wholly ignorant of one another. Thus, the debt to the Romans cannot be overestimated for abolishing this abomination, in which slaying a man was deemed a most religious act and eating his flesh was truly thought most beneficial."

Lucan, a Roman poet who lived from AD 39 to 65, wrote *Pharsalia* (also known as *The Civil War*), an epic poem detailing the conflict between Julius Caesar and Pompey. In Book 1, lines 450-58, he touches upon the Druids and their mysterious rites. Lucan writes:

> "To your barbarous rites and sinister ceremonies, O Druids, you have returned since weapons now lie still. To you alone it is given to know the gods and spirits of the sky, or perhaps not to know at all. You dwell in the distant, dark, and hidden groves. You say that shades of the dead do not seek the silent land of Erebus or the pallid kingdom of Dis, but that the same spirit controls the limbs in another realm. Death, if what you say is true, is but the mid-point of a long life."

Tacitus, one of Rome's greatest historians, lived from around AD 55 to 120. His work *Annals* provides a detailed account of the Roman Empire, including its conquests and interactions with various peoples. In Book 14, section 30, he describes the Roman invasion of the Druid sanctuary on the island of Mona (modern-day Anglesey, North Wales). Tacitus writes:

> "Standing on the shore was the opposing army, a dense formation of men and weapons. Women in black clothing like that of the Furies ran between the ranks. Wild-haired, they brandished torches. Around them, the Druids, lifting their hands upwards towards the sky to make frightening curses, frightened [the Roman] soldiers with this extraordinary sight. And so [the Romans] stood motionless and vulnerable as if their limbs were paralyzed. Then their commander exhorted them and they urged one another not to quake before an army of women and fanatics. They carried the ensigns forward, struck down all resistance, and enveloped them in [the enemy's own] fire. After that, a garrison was imposed on the vanquished and destroyed their groves, places of savage superstition. For they considered it their duty to spread their altars with the gore of captives and to communicate with their deities through human entrails."

Vopiscus, a Roman historian of the late 3rd and early 4th centuries, is one of the authors of the *Historia Augusta*, a collection of biographies of Roman emperors. In *Numerianus* 14, he recounts various events during the reign of Emperor Numerian. Vopiscus writes:

> "As my grandfather told me, Diocletian was once staying at an inn in the region of the Tungri tribe in Gaul. He was at the time still of lesser rank in the army. He went once to settle the day's bill for his accommodation with a Druidess. This woman said to him, 'You are excessively acquisitive and stingy with your money, Diocletian.' As a joke, he replied to that, 'I shall be more generous when I am emperor.' After those words, the Druidess responded, 'Don't joke, Diocletian, for you will be emperor when you have slain The Boar.'"

Ausonius, a Roman poet and teacher who lived around AD 395, composed *Commentaria Professorum*, a series of poems that reflect on the lives of various professors and scholars. In sections 4.7-10, he touches on the lineage of the Druids. Ausonius writes:

> "You are sprung from the Druids of Bayeux, if the report does not lie. To you is a sacred lineage, from the temple of Belenus."

> "Nor will I forget the old man named Phoebicius, who, though servant of [the Gaulish god] Belenus, received no profit thereby. Sprung, it is said, from the Druids of Armorica [Brittany], he received a chair at Bordeaux through the help of his son."

Hippolytus, a Christian theologian and writer of the early 3rd century, authored *Philosophumena* (also known as *Refutation of All Heresies*), a work that critiques various religious and philosophical beliefs. In Book 1, section 25, he discusses the influence of Pythagorean philosophy on the Druids. Hippolytus writes:

> "The Celtic Druids eagerly took up the philosophy of Pythagoras, having been introduced to the study by Zalmoxis, a Thracian slave of Pythagoras. He came to those lands after his master's death and explained to them his philosophy. The Celts hold the Druids as prophets and foretellers of future events because they can predict certain events by Pythagorean science and mathematics. The Druids also use magic."

Clement of Alexandria, an early Christian theologian who lived around AD 150 to 210, wrote *Stromata* (or *Miscellanies*), a work that explores a wide range of philosophical and theological ideas. In Book 1, sections 15.70.1-3, Clement discusses the origins of philosophy and the influence of various ancient traditions, including the Druids. Clement of Alexandria writes:

> "Alexander, in his book on the symbols of Pythagorean belief, says Pythagoras was a student of Zaratus the Assyrian, and wants us to believe that Pythagoras listened to the Galatae and Brahmins as well."

> "Thus the very useful study of philosophy flourished in the past among the barbarians, enlightening the peoples of the world, and only later coming to Greece. Most important were the prophets of the Egyptians, the Chaldeans of the Assyrians, the Druids of the Galatae, the Samnaeans of the Bactrians, the philosophers of the Celts, and the Magi of the Persians."

Valerius Maximus, a Roman historian and moralist who flourished in the early 1st century AD, authored *Factorum et Dictorum Memorabilium* (Memorable Deeds and Sayings), a collection of anecdotes intended to illustrate moral lessons. In Book 2, section 6.10, Valerius Maximus mentions the customs of the Gauls, particularly their belief in the immortality of the soul. Valerius Maximus writes:

"Having completed my discussion of this town [Massalia], an old custom of the Gauls should be mentioned: they lend money repayable in the next world, so firm is their belief in the immortality of the spirit. I would say they are fools, except what these trouser-wearers believe is the same as the doctrine of toga-wearing Pythagoras."

Livy, a renowned Roman historian who lived from 64/59 BC to AD 12/17, authored *Ab Urbe Condita* (From the Founding of the City), a monumental history of Rome. In Book 23, section 24, Livy recounts the tragic fate of Lucius Postumius and his army in Cisalpine Gaul. Livy writes:

"Lucius Postumius, consul designate, was lost together with his host in Cisalpine Gaul [in 216 BC]. He was leading his army by way of a huge forest that the Gauls call Litana ['The Broad One']. The Gauls had cut the trees to the right and left of the road in such a way that they stood if not disturbed but fell if lightly pushed. Postumius had two Roman legions that he led into the hostile country. The Gauls surrounded the wood, and when the Roman force entered the wood, they pushed the outermost trees that had been cut. These trees fell one against the other, each one having been unstable and barely attached, and piled up from either side, crushing the armament, men, and horses, so that scarcely ten men escaped. Postumius died fighting with all his strength, trying to avoid capture. The spoils stripped from his corpse and the severed head of the commander were taken by the Boii to their holiest temple. Then, after they removed the flesh from the head, they adorned the skull with gold according to their custom. They used it as a sacred vessel to give libations on holy days, and their priests and the custodians of their temple used it as a goblet."

NOTE: Livy's description of a skull being used as a cup by the Druids reflects a practice not unique to the Celts but one that was also observed with the Sythians and among cultures much further east, including those in Northwest China.

After the above sources, many of the sources from the Early Christian era are considered unreliable and mainly deal with the Druids as having prophetic powers or the ability to foresee the future. *The Book of Invasions* (Lebor Gabála Érenn) is a medieval Irish text that serves as a mytho-historical account of the origins and history of the Irish people. Compiled in the 11th century, it recounts a series of legendary invasions and settlements in Ireland by various peoples, beginning with the biblical flood and culminating in the arrival of the Gaels, the ancestors of the Irish, where it states locations associated far to the east such as the Caspian Sea and an association with the Sythians:

"At the end of a week, they came to the great promontory which extends northward from the Rhipaean Mountains. On the promontory, they found a well with the taste of wine and drank from it, causing them to sleep for three days and three nights until Caicher the druid spoke. 'Arise!' he said. 'We will not rest until we reach Ireland.' 'Where is Ireland?' asked Lamfhind, son of Agnoman. 'Farther than Scythia,' replied Caicher, 'and it is not we who will reach it but our children, three hundred years from today.'"

As for sources that could help establish a connection between the Druids and Pythagoras, much of what we know about Pythagoras himself is obscured by contradictions and varying accounts from ancient writers. However, we might consider the account of Iamblichus:

> "Twenty-two years Pythagoras remained in Egypt, pursuing closely his investigations, visiting every place famous for its teachings, every person celebrated for wisdom. Astronomy and geometry he especially studied, and he was thoroughly initiated in all the mysteries of the gods, till, having been taken captive by the soldiers of Cambyses, he was carried to Babylon. Here the Magi instructed him in their venerable knowledge, and he arrived at the summit of arithmetic, music, and other disciplines. After twelve years he returned to Samos, being then about fifty-six years of age."

During his time in Egypt, it is believed Pythagoras might have encountered Thales of Miletus, the first of the pre-Socratic philosophers, who also studied in Egypt. Diogenes Laërtius, quoting Aristoxenus, suggests that Pythagoras derived much of his moral teachings from the Delphic priestess Themistoclea, hinting at a connection to the Oracle at Delphi. Aristotle, in his *Protrepticus*, stated: "When Pythagoras was asked why humans exist, he said, "to observe the heavens", and he used to claim that he himself was an observer of nature, and it was for the sake of this that he had passed over into life." Pythagoras is also credited with being among the first to propose that the Earth is spherical and revolves around the sun.

Pythagoras' followers formed a secretive brotherhood devoted to religious and ascetic practices, likely influenced by the worship of Apollo. This group maintained the secrecy of its teachings. Though Pythagoras is widely considered by modern academia to have left no writings, his ideas are believed to have survived, particularly through the *Golden Verses of Pythagoras*, which encapsulate the core moral and philosophical tenets of the Pythagorean school.

THE GOLDEN VERSES OF PYTHAGORAS

1. First, worship the Immortal Gods as established and ordained by the Law.
2. Respect the Oath and honor the Heroes, full of goodness and light.
3. Also, honor the Terrestrial Spirits by giving them their due worship.
4. Respect your parents and closest relatives.
5. Among the rest of humanity, make friends with those who distinguish themselves by their virtue.
6. Always listen to their gentle advice and follow their virtuous and useful actions.
7. Avoid hating your friend for a minor fault.
8. Understand that power is closely linked to necessity.

9. Know that these things are as I have told you; and train yourself to overcome these passions:--

10. First, gluttony, laziness, sensuality, and anger.

11. Do nothing evil, whether in the presence of others or privately;

12. Above all, respect yourself.

13. Next, practice justice in your actions and words.

14. Avoid behaving irrationally or without reason.

15. Always remember that it is destined for all men to die.

16. The fortunes of life are uncertain; they can be gained or lost.

17. Regarding all calamities men suffer by divine fortune,

18. Endure your fate with patience, whatever it may be, and never complain about it.

19. Do your best to remedy it.

20. Remember that fate does not send the greatest portion of misfortunes to good men.

21. Among men, there are many kinds of reasoning, both good and bad;

22. Do not admire them too easily or reject them outright.

23. If falsehoods are presented, hear them with patience and arm yourself with endurance.

24. Always observe what I am about to tell you:--

25. Let no one, by words or deeds, ever lead you astray.

26. Do not be enticed to say or do what is not beneficial for you.

27. Consult and deliberate before you act, so you may avoid foolish actions.

28. It is the part of a miserable person to speak and act without reflection.

29. Do what will not cause you regret later or make you repent.

30. Never do anything you do not understand.

31. Learn all that you should know, and by this means, you will lead a pleasant life.

32. Do not neglect the health of your body;

33. Give it food and drink in due measure, and exercise as needed.

34. By measure, I mean what will not inconvenience you.

35. Accustom yourself to a lifestyle that is neat and decent without luxury.

36. Avoid all things that may cause envy.

37. Do not be wasteful out of season, like one who does not know what is decent and honorable.

38. Neither be greedy nor miserly; a balanced measure is excellent in these matters.

39. Do only the things that cannot harm you, and deliberate before doing them.

40. Never let sleep close your eyelids after going to bed,

41. Until you have examined all your actions of the day with reason.

42. Where have I done wrong? What have I done? What have I left undone that I ought to have done?

43. If in this examination you find that you have done wrong, reprimand yourself severely for it;

44. And if you have done good, rejoice.

45. Practice thoroughly all these things; meditate on them well; you should love them with all your heart.

46. They will guide you to the way of divine virtue.

47. I swear by him who has transmitted the Sacred Quaternion into our souls, the source of nature, whose cause is eternal.

48. Never begin any work without first praying to the gods to accomplish it.

49. Once you have made this habit familiar,

50. You will understand the constitution of the Immortal Gods and of men.

51. You will know how far different beings extend and what contains and binds them together.

52. You will also know that, according to the Law, the nature of this universe is uniform in all things,

53. So you will not hope for what you should not hope; nothing in this world will be hidden from you.

54. You will realize that men bring misfortunes upon themselves voluntarily, by their own free choice.

55. Unhappy they are! They neither see nor understand that their good is near them.

56. Few know how to free themselves from their misfortunes.

57. Such is the fate that blinds mankind and takes away their senses.

58. They roll to and fro like huge cylinders, always oppressed with countless ills.

59. Fatal strife, innate in them, pursues them everywhere, tossing them about; they do not perceive it.

60. Instead of provoking it, they should avoid it by yielding.

61. Oh! Zeus, our Father! if You would deliver men from all the evils that oppress them,

62. Show them the spirit they use.

63. But take courage; the race of man is divine.

64. Sacred nature reveals the most hidden mysteries to them.

65. If she imparts her secrets to you, you will easily perform all that I have ordained for you.

66. By healing your soul, you will free it from all evils and afflictions.

67. Abstain from the foods forbidden in purifications and the deliverance of the soul;

68. Make a just distinction of them, and examine all things well.

69. Always let yourself be guided by the understanding that comes from above, which ought to hold the reins.

70. When, after shedding your mortal body, you arrive at the purest Ether,

71. You shall be a god, immortal, incorruptible, and Death shall have no more dominion over you.

REFERENCES

1. Pausanias. *Description of Greece*. 5. 7. 8.
2. Herodotus. *Histories*. 4.32.
3. Strabo. *Geographica*. 11.4.3.
4. Clement of Alexandria. *Stromata*. iv. xxi.
5. Clement of Alexandria. *Protrepticus*. II.
6. Callimachus. *Hymn IV to Delos*. 292.
7. Asen Bondzhev, Ancient Sources about Hyperborea
8. Mallory, J. P.; Adams, Douglas Q., eds. (1997). *Encyclopedia of Indo-European Culture*. London & Chicago: Fitzroy Dearborn. ISBN 978-1-884964-98-5.
9. Mallory, J. P. (2006). *The Oxford Introduction to Proto-Indo-European and the Proto-Indo-European World*. Oxford: Oxford University Press. ISBN 978-0-19-928791-8.
10. West, Martin L. (2007). *Indo-European Poetry and Myth*. Oxford: Oxford University Press. ISBN 978-0-19-928075-9.
11. *"Wikipedia: The Free Encyclopedia."* Wikimedia Foundation. [2024].
12. Dumezil, Georges (1973). *Mythes et dieux des Indo-Européens*. Flammarion.
13. Mallory, J. P.; Adams, Douglas Q., eds. (1997). *Encyclopedia of Indo-European Culture*. London & Chicago: Fitzroy Dearborn. ISBN 978-1-884964-98-5.
14. Mallory, J. P. (2006). *The Oxford Introduction to Proto-Indo-European and the Proto-Indo-European World*. Oxford: Oxford University Press. ISBN 978-0-19-928791-8.
15. West, Martin L. (2007). *Indo-European Poetry and Myth*. Oxford: Oxford University Press. ISBN 978-0-19-928075-9.
16. Watkins, Calvert (1995). *How to Kill a Dragon: Aspects of Indo-European Poetics*. Oxford University Press. ISBN 978-0-19-508595-2.
17. Dumezil, Georges (1973). *Mythes et dieux des Indo-Européens*. Flammarion.
18. Mallory, J. P.; Adams, Douglas Q., eds. (1997). *Encyclopedia of Indo-European Culture*. London & Chicago: Fitzroy Dearborn. ISBN 978-1-884964-98-5.
19. West, Martin L. (2007). *Indo-European Poetry and Myth*. Oxford: Oxford University Press. ISBN 978-0-19-928075-9.
20. Dumézil, Georges (1970). *Archaic Roman Religion*. Chicago: University of Chicago Press. ISBN 978-0-226-16923-0.
21. Lincoln, Bruce (1991). *Death, War, and Sacrifice: Studies in Ideology and Practice*. Chicago: University of Chicago Press. ISBN 978-0-226-48197-4.
22. Birrell, Anne (1999). *Chinese Mythology: An Introduction*. Johns Hopkins University Press. ISBN 978-0-8018-6183-9.
23. Christie, Anthony (1968). *Chinese Mythology*. Feltham: Hamlyn Publishing. ISBN 978-0-600-00620-2.
24. Eberhard, Wolfram (1967). *The Local Cultures of South and East China*. E.J. Brill. ISBN 978-90-04-04520-2.
25. Yuan, Haiwang (2006). *The Magic Lotus Lantern and Other Tales from the Han Chinese*. Westport: Libraries Unlimited. ISBN 978-1-59158-294-6.
26. Werner, E. T. C. (1922). *Myths and Legends of China*. London: George G. Harrap & Co.
27. Grebennikov, Viktor S. *My World*.
28. Mair, Victor H. (1998). *The Bronze Age and Early Iron Age Peoples of Eastern Central Asia* (2 vols). Washington, D.C.: Institute for the Study of Man. ISBN 978-0-941694-63-8.
29. Mair, Victor H. (2000). *Mummies of the Tarim Basin*. Archaeology (March/April 2000).
30. Barber, Elizabeth Wayland (1999). *The Mummies of Ürümchi*. London: Macmillan. ISBN 978-0-393-32019-0.

31. Mallory, J. P., & Mair, Victor H. (2000). *The Tarim Mummies: Ancient China and the Mystery of the Earliest Peoples from the West*. London: Thames & Hudson. ISBN 978-0-500-05101-6.

32. Chen, Jianli, et al. (2021). "The Genomic Origins of the Bronze Age Tarim Basin Mummies". *Nature* 599: 256–261.

33. "Subeshi Culture." *Wikipedia, The Free Encyclopedia*

34. *"Hyperborea" Wikipedia, The Free Encyclopedia*

35. *"The Tarim Mummies" Wikipedia, The Free Encyclopedia*

36. *Gardiner, Sir Alan.* The Royal Canon of Turin. *Griffith Institute, Ashmolean Museum, 1959.*

37. *Redford, Donald B. Pharaonic King-Lists, Annals, and Day-Books: A Contribution to the Study of the Egyptian Sense of History. Benben Publications, 1986. ISBN 0-920168-07-0.*

38. *von Beckerath, Jürgen. Handbuch der ägyptischen Königsnamen. 2nd edition. Münchner Ägyptologische Studien 49, Mainz am Rhein, 1999. ISBN 3-8053-2591-6.*

39. *Wilkinson, Toby A. H. Early Dynastic Egypt. Routledge, 1999. ISBN 0-415-18633-1.*

40. *Budge, E. A. Wallis. The Gods of the Egyptians: Studies in Egyptian Mythology. Dover Publications, 1969 (reprint of the 1904 edition). ISBN 0-486-22055-9.*

41. *Wilkinson, Richard H. The Complete Gods and Goddesses of Ancient Egypt. Thames & Hudson, 2003. ISBN 0-500-05120-8.*

42. *Hart, George. A Dictionary of Egyptian Gods and Goddesses. Routledge, 1986. ISBN 0-415-05909-7.*

43. *Koch, John T., and John Carey, editors. The Celtic Heroic Age: Literary Sources for Ancient Celtic Europe and Early Ireland and Wales. Celtic Studies Publications, 2000. ISBN 1-891271-04-0.*

44. *Copenhaver, Brian P. (Translator). Hermetica: The Greek Corpus Hermeticum and the Latin Asclepius in a New English Translation, with Notes and Introduction. Cambridge University Press, 1992. ISBN 0-521-42543-3.*

45. *Fowden, Garth. The Egyptian Hermes: A Historical Approach to the Late Pagan Mind. Princeton University Press, 1993. ISBN 0-691-02498-7.*

46. *Hornung, Erik. The Secret Lore of Egypt: Its Impact on the West. Cornell University Press, 2001. ISBN 0-8014-8616-9.*

47. *Faivre, Antoine, and Rhone, Jacob. The Golden Fleece and Alchemy. SUNY Press, 1992. ISBN 0-7914-0691-X.*

48. *Bolton, J. (1962). Aristeas of Proconnesus. Oxford: Clarendon Press.*

49. *Budelmann, F. (2013). Alcman's Nightscapes (Frs. 89 and 90 PMGF). Harvard Studies in Classical Philology, 107, 35-53.*

50. *Bridgman, T. (2005). Hyperboreans: Myth and history in Celtic-Hellenic contacts. Routledge.*

51. *Diels, H., & Kranz, W. (1966). Die Fragmente der Vorsokratiker. Dublin: Weidmann.*

52. *Fleischer, K. (2019). Die älteste Liste der Könige Spartas: Pherekydes von Athen (PHerc. 1788, col. 1). ZPE 208, 1-24.*

53. *Gagné, R. (2021). Cosmography and the idea of Hyperborea in Ancient Greece: A philology of worlds. Cambridge: Cambridge University Press.*

54. *Joorde, R. (2016). Hecataeus of Abdera and his work "On the Hyperboreans" (about 300 BC): The fragments with a historical commentary. Retrieved 11 March 2023 from https://www.academia.edu/27786980/Hecataeus_of_Abdera_and_his_work_On_the_Hyperboreans_about_300_BC_T he_fragments_with_a_historical_commentary_2016.*

55. *Mette, H. (1952). Pytheas von Massalia. Berlin: de Gruyter.*

56. *Murray, O. (1970). Hecataeus of Abdera and pharaonic kingship. The Journal of Egyptian Archaeology, 56, 141-171.*

57. *Page, D. (1962). Poetae Melici Graeci. Oxford University Press.*

58. *Romm, J. (1989). Herodotus and mythic geography: The case of the Hyperboreans. Transactions of the American Philological Association, 119, 97-113.*

59. *Roseman, C. (1994). Pytheas of Massalia: On the ocean. Text, translation and commentary. Chicago: Ares Publishers.*

60. *Strauss Clay, J. (2006). The politics of Olympus. Form and meaning in the major Homeric hymns, 2nd edition. Bristol Classical Press.*

61. *Stichtenoth, D. (1959). Pytheas von Marseille. Über das Weltmeer: die Fragmente. Köln: Böhlau.*

62. *West, M. (1972). Iambi et elegi Graeci, Vol. II. Oxford University Press.*

63. *West, M. (2003). Homeric hymns. Homeric apocrypha. Lives of Homer. Cambridge: Harvard University Press.*

ALSO AVAILABLE ON KINDLE & FREE TO READ ON KINDLE UNLIMITED:

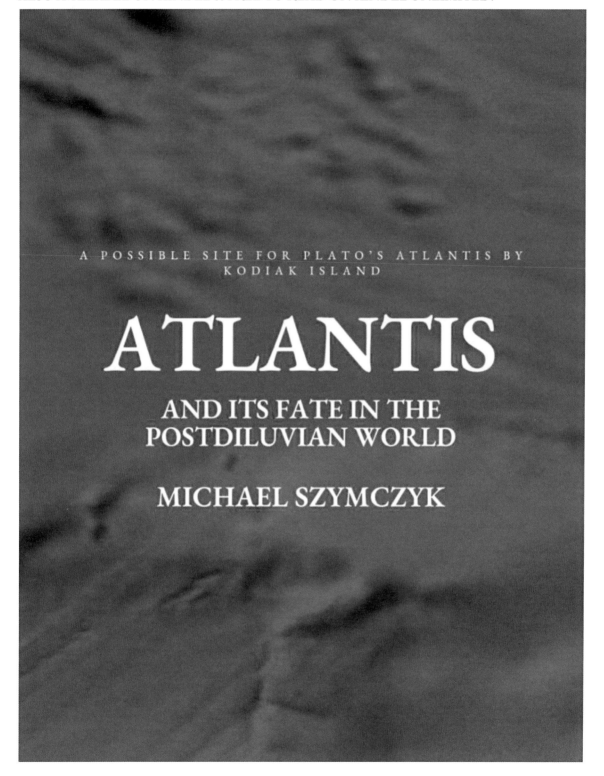

A POSSIBLE SITE FOR PLATO'S ATLANTIS BY KODIAK ISLAND

ATLANTIS

AND ITS FATE IN THE POSTDILUVIAN WORLD

MICHAEL SZYMCZYK

About the Author

Michael Szymczyk is a versatile and prolific independent filmmaker, photographer, philosopher, and novelist. He has written and directed six feature films: *Scent, Eaters of the Dead, SARS-29, Journey to the End of the Night, Night of the Skinwalkers,* and *The Reality of Time.* His literary works include the thought-provoking *Atlantis & Its Fate in the Postdiluvian World: A Possible Site for Plato's Atlantis by Kodiak Island, Independent Filmmaking 101, German 101, French 101, Toilet: The Novel, Tristan MacArthur in the 36th Century, Ancient Philosophy 101,* and *Cinematography 101.*

Michael's first novel received notable mentions in various newspapers:

- "Another candidate for the canon?" - Mike Thomas, *Chicago Sun-Times*
- "Szymczyk is smart." - Mark Eberhardt, *The Kansas City Star*